# THE LOG OF THE PANTHON

George Flavell (standing, right) and companions aboard the sloop *Examiner*, April, 1894, at Yuma, Arizona, on the lower Colorado River. The buildings of old Fort Yuma can be seen on the bluffs across the river in California. Marston Collection, Huntington Library, San Marino, California.

*An Account of an 1896 River Voyage
from Green River, Wyoming to Yuma, Arizona
through the Grand Canyon*

by
George F. Flavell

edited by
Neil B. Carmony and David E. Brown

Pruett Publishing    Boulder, Colorado    1987

1  2  3  4  5  6  7  8  9

Design by Linda Seals

LIBRARY OF CONGRESS CATALOGING-IN-PUBLICATION DATA

Flavell, George F., 1864-1901?
  The log of the Panthon.

  Bibliography: p.
  Includes index.
  1. Green River (Wyo.-Utah)–Description and
travel.  2. Grand Canyon (Ariz.)–Description and
travel.  3. Colorado River (Colo.-Mex.)–Description
and travel. Flavell, George F., 1864-1901?–
Journeys–Green River (Wyo.-Utah)  I. Carmony, Neil B.
II. Brown, David E. (David Earl), 1938-     .  III. Title.
F767.G7F55  1987  917.8      87-9649
ISBN 0-87108-732-4 (pbk.)

# CONTENTS

*To Mildred Flavell Michaelis
who preserved her uncle's logbook for half a century.*

# FOREWORD

Once a river rat, always a river rat. At least that has been my experience, as I have traveled down portions of the Green and Colorado rivers six different times and through the Grand Canyon twice. It was therefore a great pleasure for me to read the "Log of the Panthon" which describes the trip made in 1896 by George F. Flavell and Ramón Montéz.

It is a very interesting account, partly because the logbook, or diary, kept by Flavell remained hidden for so many years. It was only through the continued efforts of the late Dock Marston (probably the foremost authority on Western river travel) that the "Log" came to light.

What a thrill to read the detailed description of the trip, as these men went through rapid after rapid, put the boat back together I don't know how many times, traversed the most dangerous rapids for the first time in history, and made it all the way through the Grand Canyon with Flavell himself finally winding up at Yuma, Arizona. This is an important addition to the literature of the Colorado River and travel on it. I urge everyone who has ever heard the murmur of quiet water, the roar of a rapid, or the beautiful quiet of nighttime in a canyon to read this book. I am confident that you will find reading it to be the wonderful experience that I did.

Barry Goldwater
July 8, 1986

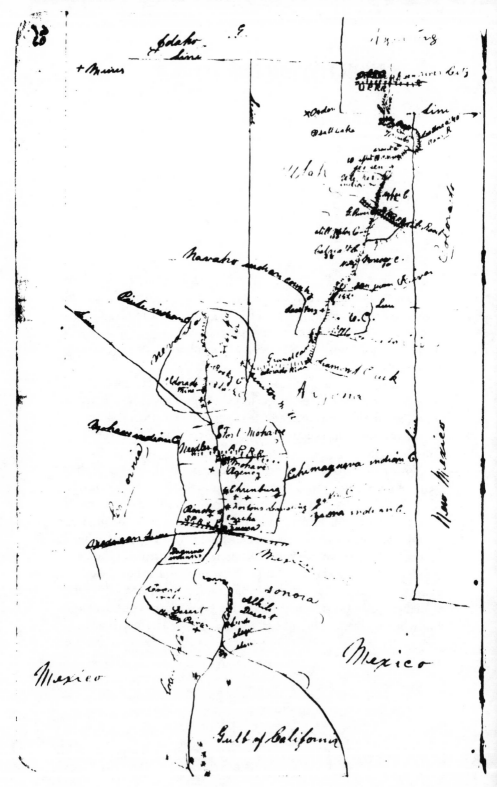

The Southwest as drawn by George Flavell.

# INTRODUCTION

By 1950, only about 100 people had traversed the Grand Canyon of the Colorado by boat. Owing to the rise of commercial river trips, during the next 35 years more than a quarter of a million people would make this fabulous journey. The popularity of challenging the rapids of the Colorado River in the depths of this greatest of canyons continues unabated.

Most of these latter-day river runners have been vacationers riding the rapids aboard boats supplied and manned by professional guides. The stark, almost overwhelming beauty of the Grand Canyon, together with the savage power of the river, made their two weeks on the water an unforgettable adventure not to be duplicated elsewhere in the world. Yet, not one in a thousand of these river runners had heard the names of the two men who pioneered white water boating on the Colorado for sport: George F. Flavell and Ramón Montéz.

On August 27, 1896, Flavell and Montéz set out from the town of Green River, Wyoming, aboard a 15-1/2-foot wooden boat named the *Panthon* with, in Flavell's words, "the intention of running down Green River into the Colorado River and on down through the Grand Canyon to Yuma." Sixty-five days later the *Panthon* exited the Grand Canyon. The men had run all but six of the hundreds of rapids that they had encountered and had completed the 1,000-mile trip without a single upset of their boat or dunking of the crew. Upon reaching Yuma, Arizona, another 500 miles downstream, George Flavell explained to a reporter for the *Arizona Sentinel* his reasons for undertaking such a formidable journey: "First, for the adventure; second, to see what so few people have seen; third, to hunt and trap; fourth, to examine the perpendicular walls of rock for gold." Flavell and Montéz were the first individuals to traverse the Grand Canyon by water who were not paid members of a government or business sponsored expedition.

The success of Flavell and Montéz in their bout with the wild rapids was reported briefly in the local press and the fact that they made the trip has long been known to historians of travel on the Green and Colorado rivers. However, the amazing details of their awesome feat have, until now, remained obscure. Unlike many river adventurers who would follow in their wake, neither Flavell nor Montéz sought to publicize his exploits. After cascading perilously through 1,000 miles of wilderness canyons, Ramón Montéz quietly left the Colorado River never to be heard of again. Some four years after completing the trip, George Flavell died unexpectedly in Mexico. The notebook containing his *Log of the Panthon* was sent to relatives in the East where for 50 years it was preserved as a family keepsake, its existence unknown to others. George Flavell's log of this epic voyage is published here for the first time.

## *Previous Expeditions*

Flavell and Montéz were not the first boatmen to explore the canyons of the Green and Colorado rivers. Much of the Green River was explored in the early 1800s by beaver trappers in crude "bullboats" made of hides stretched over wooden frames. Names and dates, carved here and there in lonely canyon recesses, testify to the visits of these mountain men. None, however, dared to enter the Grand Canyon proper, or at least none lived to tell about it.

The most famous name associated with the Green and Colorado rivers is that of Major John Wesley Powell, Civil War veteran, geologist, ethnologist, wilderness explorer, and later, the second director of the U.S. Geological Survey. In 1869 Powell led a government and university funded expedition of ten men in four boats from Green River, Wyoming, to the junction of the Virgin and Colorado rivers. Their purpose was to explore and map this almost totally unknown part of the American West. Powell and his men would thus be the first to ride the waters of the Colorado through the Grand Canyon, and his account of this arduous journey is a classic of exploration literature. In 1871–72 he led a second expedition down these forbidding rivers. The rough outline of the Southwest canyon country was now known to the outside world. The names in use today for all of the canyons of the Green River and those of the Colorado River from Cataract Canyon to the Grand Canyon (as well as the names of many lesser geographical features of the region) are those given them by members of the Powell expeditions.

Nearly two decades were to elapse before another expedition dared to challenge the rapids of the Colorado. In the late 1880s a railroad was proposed to run from Grand Junction, Colorado, down the Colorado River through the Grand Canyon to the Gulf of California, a distance of 1,200 miles. At that time it was difficult to procure coal on the Pacific Coast and it was thought that this "water-level" road, crossing no mountains, would be profitable in bringing coal from Colorado to California. A company was organized with Frank M. Brown as president, and surveys of the upper part of the river were begun in the spring of 1889. The chief engineer of the railroad survey was Robert Brewster Stanton. The difficulties encountered in conducting the survey through Cataract Canyon in southern Utah were enormous. The boats were not suitable for the river work, and it was decided to delay the survey of the Grand Canyon. A reconnaissance of the river below Lee's Ferry was attempted, however, and after proceeding about 12 miles, one of the boats capsized and Frank Brown was drowned. A few days later two other members of the party were lost in the river. After this second disaster, Stanton and the remainder of his crew cached their supplies and climbed out of Marble Canyon in July, 1889.

Still dedicated to this bizarre project, Stanton reorganized, and in December, 1889, set off with a new party of 12 men in three boats to continue the railroad survey. Equipped this time with cork life preservers, the survey party continued on through the Grand Canyon without further loss of life, reaching the mouth of the Colorado River in April, 1890. Stanton's account of his survey of the Grand Canyon, "Through the Grand Cañon of the Colorado," appeared in *Scribner's Magazine* in November, 1890, and it was this article that inspired Flavell and Montéz to test their skill against the punishing rapids six years later. Needless to say, Stanton's railroad was never built.

## Discovery of the Log

Most of what is known about George Flavell and the voyage of the *Panthon* is the result of historical research by the late Otis "Dock" Marston, an interesting Colorado River personality in his own right.

## Index

## Preface

This! Book! was written more! for
My own amusement. than any
ing else. no! apoligy is entered wha
for bad writing. spelling or compo
Education! like any thing else, when
used. gets moth eaten, or grows rusty
this Book written upon. a Slab of M
Walnut, or Mohogony! but was he
my arm or knee.          George, 

A page from Flavell's logbook.

In 1942, at the age of 48, Dock Marston rode the waters of the Colorado through the Grand Canyon for the first time, a paying passenger on an early guided commercial trip. He was captivated by the experience. Each summer thereafter, Marston could be found on the river, battling the raging rapids. Despite his age, he became an expert white water boatman.

Marston's fascination with river running soon gave rise to another passion—research into the history of fast water navigation on the Green and Colorado rivers. Over the years Dock Marston spared neither time nor expense in assembling an enormous collection of important riverine documents and photographs. It was he who located Flavell's journal containing the *Log of the Panthon* in the late 1940s. The battered old notebook was then in the possession of Mildred Flavell Michaelis, George Flavell's niece who was living in New Jersey.

Surprisingly, the obscurity of Flavell and Montéz did not end with the discovery of the *Log*. Marston intended to incorporate Flavell's account into a massive history of white water boating on the Green and Colorado rivers that he had begun to write. An entire chapter was to be devoted to George Flavell, the "Master Mariner," the early boatman whom Marston most admired. Unfortunately, Dock Marston was not a skillful writer and his book remained in draft form at the time of his death in 1979. His canyonlands papers are now housed at the Huntington Library, San Marino, California.

## George Flavell

George F. Flavell was born about 1864 in the farming village of Jefferson, New Jersey. His father, Jeremiah, and his mother, Anna Victoria, eventually had six children, three girls and three boys. George was not cut out for the farming life and he left home while in his early teens.

Almost nothing is known about George Flavell's activities during the next ten years. He lived in Philadelphia for a time; became an expert sailor and shipwright; went west to California; and took up commercial hunting and trapping to make a living. Out West he began to occasionally go by the name of Clark. The reason for Flavell's use of an alias is not known, but there does not appear to have been anything sinister involved. In any case, many people in California and Arizona knew George Flavell as George Clark or as "Clark the Trapper."

About 1890, George Flavell, now joined by a younger brother, Roland, began plying his trade as a trapper on the lower Colorado River. Their special haunt was the Colorado Delta south of Yuma, Arizona, then a thousand square miles of uninhabited marshy wilderness, a haven for beaver, waterfowl, and other wildlife—truly a hunter's paradise. Although Mexican territory, there was no official Mexican presence in the Delta, and the Flavells roamed the numerous lagoons and sloughs without regard to the international boundary. They trapped beaver for their pelts (worth from $2.00 to $8.00 apiece at the time), coyotes for their scalps (redeemable in California for a $5.00 bounty), and shot water birds for their plumes, which were in great demand by milliners. The men worked the river from the Gulf of California to the foot of the Grand Canyon. Their home was their camp and they possessed nothing that couldn't be transported in a small skiff. The cooler months were spent on the river, the broiling heat of the desert summers was avoided by visiting the California coast.

Roland Flavell returned to New Jersey early in 1893, where he settled down and raised a family. George Flavell remained in the Southwest. In the spring of 1893, he finished building the *Dart*, a 30-foot, flat-bottomed, two-masted ship, and sailed single-handed from Yuma to Guaymas, Sonora, and back, a round trip of about 1,000 miles. This was considered quite a feat by those familiar with the tempestuous Gulf.

The Flavells were among the last of an interesting breed of Americans—the professional hunters. Their lineage goes back to the frontiersmen who crossed the Appalachian Mountains in the late 1700s and includes the "mountain men" who scoured the West for beaver in the early 1800s. Also included are the buffalo hunters of the 1860s and '70s, the market hunters who supplied meat to the mining camps of the Rockies, and finally the plume hunters of the 1890s. By the turn of the century, encroaching civilization, dwindling wildlife populations, and federal and state game laws put an end to the American professional hunter. These men still live in the American imagination as our most powerful symbols of vigor, freedom, and self-reliance.

But one photograph of George Flavell is known to exist and it only shows him at a distance (see frontispiece). He was about medium height and slender. By the 1890s he had acquired a number of tattoos and practiced the technique of applying them; a kit of tattooing needles and ink was always among his Spartan possessions. Contrary to what one might expect of a backwoodsman, George Flavell was, by all accounts, a mild mannered fellow, not prone to heavy drinking or brawling, and not given to the use of rough speech. His writings, which include several poems, reveal that he was a man of considerable sensitivity. Despite his lonely lifestyle, he enjoyed the company of others, and loved to swap yarns and gossip with those he unexpectedly met in the wilderness. He possessed a lively sense of humor. George Flavell was a prolific letter writer but, unfortunately, little of his correspondence survives.

## The Tiburon Island Tragedy

An incident occurred in the spring of 1894 that would torment George Flavell for the rest of his life. Flavell and four companions proposed to spend several weeks exploring the islands and the coast of the upper Gulf of California aboard the *Examiner*, a 32-foot sloop that Flavell remodeled from a clumsy houseboat. The expedition was organized by R. E. L. Robinson, a free-lance journalist who was interested in the mining potential of the region. Besides Flavell and Robinson, the crew included Charles Cowell, Morgan O'Brien, and James Logan. The *Examiner* left Yuma, Arizona, in mid-April and cruised down the Colorado to the Gulf.

The voyage proceeded in a leisurely fashion—the men hunted feral hogs in the delta's marshes, fished and speared turtles in the bays, and landed at various points to prospect and stalk bighorn sheep in the rugged coastal mountains. After several petty disputes with Robinson, Cowell abandoned the *Examiner* at Los Angeles Bay on the Baja California coast and boarded a ship bound for Guaymas, Sonora.

On May 25, the *Examiner* reached the northern end of Tiburon Island off the coast of Sonora, the largest island in the Gulf and the stronghold of the Seri Indians. The adventurers dropped anchor a few hundred feet offshore opposite an Indian village on the beach. George Flavell went ashore in a skiff to parley, but as the Seris had an evil reputation and were thought by some to be cannibals, he approached with caution. Flavell had acquired a vocabulary of "border Mexican" and found that several of the Indians spoke enough "Mexican" for them to communicate. The Seris seemed surprisingly friendly. One of the men produced a paper issued by authorities at Hermosillo, the capital of Sonora, stating that the bearer had been appointed "governor" of the island and spokesman for its inhabitants. Their apprehensions considerably allayed, the other Americans came ashore and inquired if there was any game on the island. The Seris replied that there were many large deer in the mountains of the island, and Robinson and Logan made arrangements to go hunting with some of the Indians the next day.

On the morning of the 26th, Robinson and Logan took the expedition's two rifles and set out with five of the Seri on their hunt. The Indians were armed with some old rifles they said they obtained through trade with the Yaquis. Flavell stayed in the village and O'Brien, who had been sick for much of the voyage, remained aboard the *Examiner*. After about two hours, Flavell heard shots and then shouts coming from a nearby canyon. The Indians on the beach became agitated and started to flee to the foothills. Flavell, armed with only a pistol, realized that trouble was afoot and jumped into the skiff and rowed out to the sloop. More shots were heard, and what sounded like James Logan calling for help; then silence. Morgan O'Brien got out the shotgun, the only other weapon on board, and the men waited and watched, hoping that their companions would appear on the beach, but expecting to see a flotilla of Seri canoes coming to attack the becalmed *Examiner*.

Flavell and O'Brien kept watch throughout the afternoon, but nothing more was heard and no one was seen. The next morning a breeze came up and the two men set sail, slowly heading south. They reached the port city of Guaymas, Sonora, about 100 miles south of Tiburon, on May 31, where they reported to the Mexican authorities that Robinson and Logan had been killed by the Seris.

The public response to the reported tragedy took Flavell by surprise. The initial reaction in Arizona was one of skepticism. Robinson had the reputation of occasionally fabricating flamboyant tales to sell a story, and many felt that the Seri attack was a hoax: Robinson would soon appear with a hair-raising account of how he had escaped from the cannibals. When it became apparent that something untoward had indeed befallen the two Americans, suspicion fell on Flavell and O'Brien. Might they not have robbed and murdered their companions and conveniently blamed the Seris? However, those who knew the two men quickly vouched that they were honest and reliable, not the sort to commit such a crime. When at last Flavell and O'Brien's account of the happenings on Tiburon became accepted as true, the men still received little sympathy. Could they not have done more to help their embattled comrades? Moreover, the Mexican officials scolded the Americans for going onto the island when they knew the Seris could be dangerous.

Flavell was stung by these accusations and resolved to vindicate himself. His retreat to the sloop may not have been particularly courageous, but it was definitely prudent. Greatly outnumbered, he and O'Brien had sailed to Guaymas expecting help, not harassment. They had assumed the Mexican Government would promptly investigate the incident and punish the treacherous Indians. A month after the killings had been reported, the commandant at Guaymas dispatched a contingent of 50 soldiers, with Flavell as guide, to examine the scene of the crime. The Mexicans spent a few hours in a cursory search of the vicinity where the Americans were thought to have been killed, found nothing – no remains of Logan and Robinson, no Indians – and promptly returned home. As far as the Mexicans were concerned, the case was closed. George Flavell was disgusted by this perfunctory performance. He sold the *Examiner* at Guaymas and returned to the United States.

The Tiburon tragedy continued to be debated in the American press for several months. Flavell and others succeeded in persuading the U.S. State Department to file an inquiry with the Mexican government, but nothing more was done. Eventually the Mexican officials became sufficiently annoyed with Flavell's protests to advise him to stay out of Mexico. George Flavell felt abused by the Mexican government and ignored by his own. Gradually the incident became an old story and was forgotten by the public.

George Flavell preserved the bound notebook in which R. E. L. Robinson had kept the log of the voyage of the *Examiner*, and two years later used this notebook to record his adventures on the Green and Colorado rivers. On September 5, 1896, while relaxing on the bank of the Green River in Colorado, George Flavell briefly summarized his activities since the Tiburon debacle: "I have been in Washington hunting; been sailing on the Pacific Coast; shipped once for Africa, but by a lucky scratch got off of the vessel; and have been trapping on the Colorado. Have not been since across the Mexican line."

### Ramón Montéz

Next to nothing is known about Ramón Montéz, George Flavell's companion on the Green–Colorado river trip. Montéz was evidently a resident of San Fernando, a small town near Los Angeles. Remarks in Flavell's log indicate that he was a "tenderfoot," unskilled in the techniques of wilderness travel. In short, Montéz was Flavell's passenger on their perilous voyage. Nonetheless, Ramón Montéz must have made up in courage what he lacked in experience. After leaving the Colorado River at Needles, California, Ramón Montéz disappeared from history.

## Flavell and Montéz Prepare for the River Trip

In early August, 1896, George Flavell and Ramón Montéz left San Fernando, California, by rail, and arrived at Green River, Wyoming, on about August 17. The adventurers immediately set about building a boat in which to navigate the wild river that flowed past their camp. Flavell was an expert with saw and plane, and the small craft was completed in eight days. They christened their creation the *Panthon*. As to the meaning of this name, we have not a clue.

Of necessity the men traveled light. Their food supplies consisted of the standard back country fare of the day: beans, bacon, flour for making bread, and coffee, to be supplemented with game killed along the way. A rifle, pistol, and several beaver traps were stowed away, along with an axe, knives, cooking utensils, a few blankets and a tarpaulin or two. A large coil of rope was put on board. Flavell wisely included materials with which to make repairs to the *Panthon*: some extra planks, caulking, nails and other hardware, and woodworking tools. With Robinson's notebook and Stanton's Grand Canyon article in hand, the intrepid river runners were ready. There were no life preservers on board.

## *The* Panthon

George Flavell does not describe his boat in detail. What is known about the *Panthon* is due to the inquisitiveness of the irrepressible Robert Brewster Stanton. Although Stanton never built his canyonlands railroad, he maintained a keen interest in the region. Somehow he heard about the Flavell–Montéz expedition and wrote to his friend, John Hislop, of Green River, Utah, to learn some of the details. Hislop, who had served as Stanton's chief assistant on the Colorado River surveys of 1889–90, sent him the following letter dated October 4, 1896:

Green River (City), Wyoming. The Green River is in the foreground, the Union Pacific Railroad bridge across the river is at the left, and Sentinel Rock is in the background. A. C. Veatch, 1908, U.S.G.S., Denver, Colorado.

Dear Mr. Stanton:

Yours of the 30th received today. A week ago Saturday two prospectors from San Fernando, Cal., had dinner with us. They left Green River, Wyoming, in the boat *Panthon of Green River*, Aug. 27th.

Their boat is a flat bottomed boat with broad, square stern, two oars worked by one man in the bow who sits face to the bow and pushes on the oars. No steering or extra oars. The other man sits on the load in the stern. The oarsman sits on a box when not standing. No airtight compartments. Boat built by themselves and shod with wagon tires, etc. Have 750 feet of rope weighing 125 lbs.

Say they let the boat over four rapids above here. Stopped twice for repairs. Their object is to prospect in the Grand Canyon. Expect to reach the Needles in March. One of them was at Lerdo, Mexico, and saw our boat in 1890. They had your article (Scribner's) and said you mentioned perpendicular falls of 15 ft. I corrected that idea. We encouraged them in their effort and asked them to let us know how they got along. Their boat is very light in the bow.

Yours truly,

John Hislop

Additional notes compiled by Stanton reveal that the *Panthon* was an open boat, 15-1/2 feet long, with a five-foot beam. It had a 2×4 frame covered with tongue-and-groove planks. The bottom was double planked and reinforced with iron skids made from old wagon tires. Robert Stanton's personal papers are now at the New York Public Library. Copies of virtually all of his papers that deal with the Colorado River are in the Marston Collection at the Huntington Library, San Marino, California.

Much of the hardship and disaster that characterized the Powell and Stanton expeditions was caused by the design of their boats. Those used by Powell in 1869 were 21 feet long, round-bottomed, very heavy and difficult to maneuver. The boats initially used by Stanton were round-bottomed and too fragile to withstand the river.

The *Panthon* proved to be just what the wild rivers demanded: it was small and maneuverable; flat-bottomed for stability and shallow draft; it was stoutly constructed with plenty of freeboard to withstand the punishment of rocks and rapids; and, importantly, it was designed to allow the oarsman to face the bow, the direction of travel. The *Panthon* could have been improved, from a safety standpoint, by the addition of some watertight flotation chambers, but since the boat was never upset or swamped, this deficiency did not prove important. Skill, daring, luck, and a suitable boat allowed Flavell and Montéz to avoid both upsets and the man-killing toil of portages.

## Flavell's River Running Technique

The oarsmen of the Powell and Stanton parties sat facing the sterns of their boats with their backs to the direction of travel, in typical rowboat fashion: a poor way to negotiate a crashing rapid.

Flavell's technique of facing forward at the oars, with a clear view of approaching hazards, is by far the superior method and is now standard among white water boatmen using oar-powered craft. Nathaniel Galloway has often erroneously been credited with being the first to run the rapids of the Colorado using this "face the danger" technique. Galloway and William Richmond, two beaver trappers from Utah, successfully negotiated the Green and Colorado rivers from near Green River, Wyoming, to Needles, California, a few months *after* the Flavell–Montéz trip. The trappers used two boats built by Galloway that were similar in size and design to the

*Panthon.* The oarsmen faced the sterns of the boats, but turned them about and ran the rapids stern first. George Flavell reportedly met Galloway upon the latter's arrival at Needles in February, 1897. Flavell had been enthralled by his wilderness adventure; Galloway gruffly dismissed his river trip as being of "no profit."

### First to Run the Rapids

The most remarkable aspect of the Flavell–Montéz river odyssey is how few times they were forced to either "line" their boat through or portage their boat around rapids. Four rapids were lined in the Canyon of Lodore on the Green River in northwestern Colorado, and they lined one rapid in Cataract Canyon on the Colorado River in southern Utah. Their most impressive achievement, however, was running the rapids on the Colorado River in the Grand Canyon in Arizona. From Lee's Ferry to the Grand Wash Cliffs, a distance of 277 river miles, the Colorado River flows through the Grand Canyon's vast complex of gorges containing scores of rapids, dozens of which are extremely hazardous. Both Powell and Stanton lined and portaged many rapids during their laborious traverses of the Canyon. Flavell and Montéz ran all but Soap Creek Rapid located 11 miles downstream from Lee's Ferry. They were the first to run Hance Rapid, Lava Falls Rapid, and many of the other truly dangerous cataracts. Running the rapids rather than lining or portaging them enabled Flavell and Montéz to make the run from Lee's Ferry through the Grand Canyon in a record 14 days. Four decades would go by before a boat would pass through the Grand Canyon in less time.

Float trips through the canyons of the Green and Colorado rivers are now an everyday occurrence. Thus it is easy to overlook the enormity of Flavell and Montéz' accomplishment. They were the first and for 40 years the only adventurers to complete this riverine *jornada* trusting their lives to a single boat. Without life preservers and other boats and boatmen to help, an upset of the *Panthon* could easily have resulted in Flavell and Montéz' names being added to the long list of lives lost in the deadly rapids. They were also the first and for decades the only individuals to truly "conquer" the rapids of the Colorado. Lava Falls Rapid, first run by Flavell and Montéz in 1896, was not again successfully run until 1938! It was not until after World War II, after the river had become well known and modern river running equipment and techniques had been perfected, that running the major rapids of the Colorado was viewed as merely risky instead of extremely dangerous. Flavell and Montéz' river journey must rank as one of the outstanding feats of American wilderness travel.

## George Flavell's Last Years

Not much information has come down to us regarding George Flavell's life after his daring river journey. In the spring of 1897 he briefly captained the *Little Dick*, a gasoline-powered boat that hauled freight up and down the Colorado in the vicinity of Yuma. George Flavell married Lulu Blanche Shaffer on May 14, 1898, in Los Angeles. He was 34 years of age, she was 33. Nothing more is known about his married life.

Despite the warnings and admonishments, George Flavell returned to Mexico about 1900 on a prospecting trip. The lure of gold was too strong for the adventurous Flavell to resist. He died in Hermosillo, Sonora, in 1900 or 1901, reportedly of typhoid fever. Some family members doubted the report that he died of natural causes, in view of his previous troubles in Mexico. However, there was no evidence that George Flavell had met with foul play. He was buried near Hermosillo.

Upon his death, the Mexican authorities sent a bundle of George Flavell's personal effects to his brother and former trapping partner, Roland Flavell, who was living in New Jersey. Included was the notebook containing the record of the Tiburon Island tragedy and the Green–Colorado river triumph. Roland Flavell died in 1932 and the book passed to his daughter Mildred. Mildred Flavell Michaelis donated her uncle's logbook to the National Park Service at Grand Canyon, Arizona, in 1980.

## The Log *as Literature*

Contrary to what one might expect, the *Log of the Panthon* is *not* a collection of cursory notes and remarks—it is a literate narrative written in a lively style with considerable humor. Flavell describes the canyon country and its few human inhabitants with sensitivity and perception. This is surprising because the *Log* was written by a backwoodsman with little formal education. It is even more remarkable because the account that follows, unlike many published river journals, was written in its entirety in the wilderness with the roar of a wild river in the writer's ears. Even Major Powell's wonderful account (presented in diary form) of his historic trip down the Green and Colorado rivers was written in Washington from brief notes taken in the field. George Flavell's ability to write effectively was doubtless an inborn talent honed by letter writing (an activity in eclipse in the electronic age). Although there is no indication that he ever attempted to publish the *Log*, he clearly wrote it with readers in mind. The *Log of the Panthon* is one of the best of the Western river journals.

In preparing the *Log of the Panthon* for publication, editorial impact has been kept to a minimum. Only minor modifications have been made. Confusing spelling inconsistencies have been eliminated. Punctuation has been added when necessary to render a passage more comprehensible. Here and there an awkward construction has been slightly altered for the sake of readability. Otherwise, George Flavell's rough-hewn but engaging prose has been left intact.

## *The Rivers After the Voyage of the* Panthon

The voyage made by George Flavell and Ramón Montéz in 1896 cannot now be repeated. The twentieth century has seen dam after dam built on the Colorado and Green rivers and hundreds of miles of river and canyon inundated. The new reservoirs are the resort of water-skiers and sport fishermen, not river explorers and beaver trappers. Yet, some wild river remains and the prospects for preserving this remnant look bright. Much of the Green River is close to pristine, and the rapids still roar in the Grand Canyon even though the flow of the Colorado is controlled by Glen Canyon Dam. Below the Grand Canyon most of the Colorado is either flooded by reservoirs or flows through a straightened, canal-like channel. The rivers of the Southwest were seen by previous generations as simply too valuable a resource to leave alone. Anything less than total development was quite unthinkable. Let's hope that we have truly gained by trading the excitement and grandeur of wild rivers for hydroelectric power and irrigation water. And let's be glad that a bit of the glory of the old unfettered Green and Colorado rivers survives in the writings of men like George Flavell.

# CHAPTER I

# Green River, Wyoming, to Green River, Utah

*August 27–30, 1896.* The campfire is burning bright. We have the hindquarters of a deer in the ground cooking, and a big stew besides. As the flames of a big pitch log go up, I start the *Log of the Panthon* and time alone will tell if it will ever be finished or not.[1]

We proceeded to Green River City, Wyoming, with the intention of running down Green River into the Colorado River and on down through the Grand Canyon to Yuma. We arrived at Green River City from San Fernando, California, and began constructing a boat for the trip. It was completed in eight days, but we were compelled to wait a day or two longer for some things we were expecting from San Francisco. They arrived on the morning of the 27th and as the whistle blew for the noon hour we pushed out on what will, without doubt, be a very interesting if not dangerous trip.

We drifted along through a high, rolling country, the hills being from one to four hundred feet high and covered with a scanty growth of small shrubbery and little or no grass. We passed a few herds of cattle—at times 9/10 of them were hornless.

Nothing of note occurred till the afternoon of the 29th when, as we were drifting along, we spied three deer on a small island. We made a landing and I went to procure some venison. After getting about 30 feet from one (considering that close enough), I drew a bead on its shoulder. At the crack of the rifle it ran as though it had not been scratched and I finally concluded it had not been. Well! Then the bombardment com-

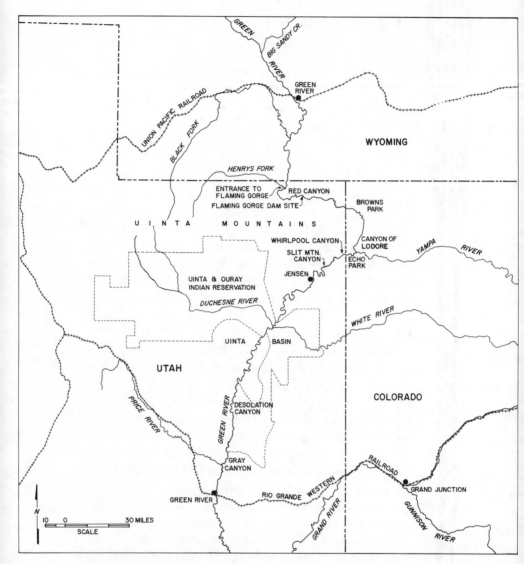

The upper Green River country, circa the 1890s.

menced. I shot no less than 12 shots, four of them at standing deer and none of them over 60 yards. The island only had about 10 acres in it and was thickly covered with willows and other brush. Ramón would run them out of the thickets and I would blaze away, always with the same result. I got after the old doe and run her off the island entirely, sending lead after her every jump, but she only went

18

faster. Well! The two of us finally run down a fawn, and got into camp as it was getting dark. Of course we did not eat any for supper!

After breakfast [on August 30], we thought we would take one more farewell look around the island before we left. Ramón took the rifle for a change, and I armed myself with the old 45 Colt. It was not long till there was a racket in the brush about 10 feet from me, and I called to Ramón to look out, that it was coming his way. I was after it red hot, with the pistol at full cock. In about five seconds I heard the rifle ring out. I was out of the brush before the report died away, and Ramón was standing over the first deer he had ever killed, sawing away on its throat. It was the same one I had shot at first the evening before. I had split its brisket and carried away part of the front leg, but did not break the bone. It also had a rip up the back about six inches long. We went back to the boat and started on down the river with a deer and a half in the boat, we having ate the other half for supper and breakfast.

At 11 A.M. six more deer were sighted on the "east coast." I lit out barefooted (as I had done on the island the day before) and after running about 1/2 mile, I stopped hunting deer and commenced picking cactus out of my feet. When I got the biggest portion out I came back to the boat and we went on, with the deer looking at us from a high ridge where they had taken refuge.

At 12 A.M. we entered Dolores Canyon [Flaming Gorge],[2] and after four hours we struck the rapids [at the head of Red Canyon]; in two hours we ran about 20, some pretty swift. They spread out so, it was hard to find a channel through and we were continually bumping boulders and, by carelessness, got hung up on one for about 1/2 hour. We had quite a time getting off. After that I was more careful, but it was impossible to avoid them all—to try to miss one was only to hit another.

Well! Now I have written up to date. It must be 10 P.M. and I guess the straw needs attending to, so good night. Progress made: 84 miles.[3]

*August 31.* 8:30 A.M. found us moving. The rapids were so thick it seemed like one continual one. At 12 A.M. we stopped for dinner and saw bear tracks on the beach, but no bear. Three beaver were seen during the day. One place the river was completely dammed up with boulders which caused a falls of four feet, the widest passage being 10 feet.[4] That was enough for the *Panthon*, so we passed on.

Island in the Green River. E. O. Beaman, 1871, U.S.G.S., Denver, Colorado.

Entrance to Flaming Gorge, Utah. E. O. Beaman, 1871, U.S.G.S., Denver, Colorado.

Later on in the afternoon Ramón was singing. All of a sudden he stopped. Everything did the same, except the load in the boat. That shot ahead. It was caused by a collision with a rock about 15 feet high. I saw I could not miss it, and so I struck it square with the stem. Ramón was sitting on the trunk in the stern of the boat, and when the collision stopped her so suddenly Ramón came on forward and skinned his knees on the seat about three feet ahead

21

of where he was sitting. It was all over in a second. The boat swung round and went on downstream, stern first.

We passed a cowboy and had a chat with him, the first person we had seen to speak to since we started. Two others had been seen at a distance on the 29th. We sighted a conglomeration of old shacks just before we camped. A man was standing in the door of one but as we drew near he disappeared, and as he appeared to be sort of *bronco* [rough], we decided not to pollute his sacred abode with our presence, so we drifted on and camped a mile or so below [probably in "Little Hole"].[5] During the day we had run 64 rapids ranging from 200 yards to one mile in length, and as high as a 12 foot fall in 400 yards. Progress made: 48 miles [actually about 20 miles].

*September 1.* After running 12 more rapids, Dolores Canyon [the Flaming Gorge–Red Canyon complex] was left behind. Its length is about 70 miles [actually about 40 miles], with a total of 96 rapids, and actual running time of 14 hours. At this stage of the water there is no danger of losing life, but many chances to lose a boat if not properly handled.[6] After leaving the canyon we entered a low, rolling country [Brown's Park] for a few miles, and then a small canyon [Swallow Canyon] some four miles long [actually two miles long] with perpendicular walls of one to two hundred feet. The water was calm and smooth as glass. Another small canyon was passed in the afternoon.

A little before sundown a mower was heard and a house was seen on the bank (we were now in Colorado). We camped just below.[7] Supper was started, but soon postponed on account of a shower. It soon ceased. Supper over, I went up to the house and had a chat. Like all the rest, they said we would leave our carcasses in Lodore Canyon (a canyon some miles below) if we entered it. Several have told us of the impossibility of even getting through, though none know what is in there or how long it is. All they know is that it is awful and that everyone who went in there stayed. I have come to the conclusion they don't know any more about it than I do. There is a canyon, that is all.

When I came back from the house there was a mist in drops as large as grapes, and when I got back to camp I found Ramón floating around in bed. I just tumbled in too and we both floated together. Progress made: 27 miles.

Ashley Falls (looking upstream) in Red Canyon, Utah. This site is now under the waters of Flaming Gorge Reservoir. E. O. Beaman, 1871, U.S.G.S., Denver, Colorado.

*September 2.* This morning everything is hung out to dry, including ourselves. I am hung out in the boat, but my pants are on the line. Consequently I am not dressed to receive company. At 9 A.M. we were drifting, and about 11 A.M. a deep gash was distinguished in the mountain ahead. We surmised what it meant: the great Lodore Canyon[8] where we entered at 2:30 P.M.

The first dash was through a ridge about a mile long with almost straight walls 3,000 feet high [The Gates of Lodore]. It was the greatest sight I had ever beheld. It was not long until it was necessary to open the coil of rope that had not been before needed, for we struck rapids that were dangerous to run on account of boulders. The boat got pretty well shook up. The keelson got knocked off, and we must be a little more careful.

Inside the Gates of Lodore. E. O. Beaman, 1871, U.S.G.S., Denver, Colorado.

The roar of rapids comes from both ways. We are camped just at the top of one [Upper Disaster Falls] which will probably be the most difficult to pass of any yet encountered. Progress made: 27 miles [actually about 18 miles].

*September 3.* Progress slow and plenty of work, with a slight mixture of excitement. Rapids were thick, rocky, and swift. Five were passed in two miles. It was necessary to lower over three, respectively 6, 10, and 18 feet. The last mentioned [Lower Disaster Falls] was a good place to bring an expedition to a close very sudden. The river came down on a curve and ran under a perpendicular wall where it had cut in, most of the river running under, the water having a fall of about 10 feet before it got to that point. When the boat's stern was only a few feet from the bluff, ready to be gobbled up should the line break, even a new 3/4 inch line looked small enough. The roar was so loud, a voice could only be heard a few feet.[9] But it was passed, and though we ate supper only two miles or less from where breakfast was disposed of, we are about 50 feet lower. If there is a place on my body as large as this sheet of paper that is not sun burnt, it must be on the inside.

*September 4.* Progress was some better today, making 30 miles [actually about 12 miles] with 29 rapids ranging from 3 to 20 feet of fall. The worst [Hell's Half Mile] required four hours hard work to pass, its length being 1/2 mile. We arrived at the mouth of Bear River [Yampa River] at sundown.

As we pulled in to camp an object was seen on the bank below which soon assumed the shape of a man. We dropped on down four or five hundred yards farther to where he was, and a curious man he was, living there in the canyon all alone. As soon as the bow of the boat touched the shore, he grabbed the rope and offered his hand and said, "Welcome to Echo Park," and asked my name. He did the same with Ramón. As soon as he saw the boat was secure, he started off after wood to make a fire. I asked him a few questions, but he seemed to take no notice to what I said. He acted so curious, I began to think he was crazy. He ate supper with us. I soon gave up all attempts to get him to answer any questions. Finally he began to talk on his own hook, and I never was more interested in my life.

Echo Park, Colorado. The Yampa River is in the foreground, the Green River is to the right. E. O. Beaman. 1871, U.S.G.S., Denver, Colorado.

He gave us his whole history, how he had been a soldier before, during, and after the [Civil] War. He had been well-to-do in Maryland. His wife died. All he had was divided between his two sons when he was forced to fly through some trouble. He went to Africa. He learned to be a sailor. He had been in the Navy, had applied for a pension, but through some mismanagement he failed to get it. And one thing he said struck me kind of forcibly. It was, "Well, I don't need their damned pension. I won't live long anyway." He is 67 years old. He expects only to live till he reaches 71, taking in consideration the hard usage he had underwent.

He talked till 11 P.M., hitting on nearly every subject from trapping to running a government, giving us all kind of advice. But the part that impressed me most was the story of his family that was broke-up during or before the War. I was afraid to make any inquiries for fear he would stop talking, but perhaps he has one or two sons today in Maryland. What would they think if they knew their old father was living alone in Lodore Canyon, Colorado, and had not ate a piece of bread for a month, or drank a cup of coffee for two weeks, when perhaps they might have bread to feed the hogs.

I went up to his camp in the bushes, and such a camp it was. His house was a kind of a sled (anyway it was on runners), just big enough for a bed, covered with a piece of canvas held up by bows about two feet high. The table was a piece of board on the ground. It made me feel lonesome as I looked at it, and I laid awake most of the night, wondering if I would pass my last days in some such place. And though he lived so far from nowhere, he was far better posted on what was going on in the world than I was.

He had a little patch of potatoes, corn, and wheat. At this time of year he lived on potatoes and corn. We were compelled to accept some potatoes. When he harvests his wheat, the heads are rubbed between the hands and ground in a coffee mill. He sung us songs, or rather parts of several. He had forgot them all and he would try one and then another. Well, it is a long story to tell.

*September 5.* We were awakened by a shot. It was fired by the old fellow. He was up before dawn, trying to kill us some meat. He had told us there were plenty of deer, and also that he had a pet buck, hoping we would spare him if we could get another. But, he being so anxious to make us a present of some meat for breakfast, he could get a shot at no other. He let blaze at his pet buck,

The hermit Pat Lynch in Echo Park, Colorado, in the 1890s. Utah State Historical Society, Salt Lake City.

but it not being quite daylight yet, he did not kill it (at least not dead). The buck gave a bound in the air and was out of sight in the brush and probably is lying dead on the mountainside somewhere now.

He showed us a ledge [ore deposit] he had on the other side of the river, we taking him over in the boat (he had none of his own). He says that if it turns out anything, part of it is ours. He is showing Ramón his potatoes and corn now, while I am writing, as it would be impossible to write when he is present. I am going to investigate Bear River this afternoon for beaver.

*September 6.* My investigation proved fruitless, and this morning, after making some exchanges, we went round the bend of the river, leaving Patrick Lynch[10] standing on the bank, where he stood watching us till the *Panthon* shot out of sight [into Whirlpool Canyon]. So we will leave him there in his mountain home, hemmed

Looking down into Whirlpool Canyon, northwestern Colorado. Colorado Historical Society, Denver.

in on all sides by high walls, where the eye of man has never, or seldom ever, seen. Four hours later the great Lodore Canyon [Lodore and Whirlpool canyons] was left behind, with its 65 roaring rapids. But ere the sun had set we were in another...Split Mountain Canyon. Progress made: 32 miles [actually about 18 miles].

*September 7.* Though short, its entire length being only 10 miles, Split Mountain Canyon used us worse than all. The rapids, numbering 21, are short and rocky. In running one, I lost control of the boat entirely. To help it along, the rowlock jumped out. We got tangled up in the boulders, first bow and then stern first, but finally we came out at the bottom. It was all done in less than a minute. Another boulder was collided with, where we resided for a few minutes until a little sleight of hand was performed to get off. In this performance no one slept.

The south end of the canyon had the opportunity of gazing on the stern of the *Panthon* at 10:30 A.M. and a high, rolling country [the Uinta Basin] was before us. We arrived at Jensen.[11] After mailing a couple of letters at the post office, we hastened on. Rainy weather overtook us, which caused some delay as well as inconvenience. Progress made: 25 miles.

*September 8–17.* The last week was passed without anything of interest—only a few Indians were seen in passing through the Ute Reservation [Uinta and Ouray Indian Reservation]. Game was scarce. In fact, nothing was to be seen but a high, rolling country with higher mountains far in the background. We had some sport shooting beaver, and with the rifle and traps combined a dozen. They were just in condition for the London market. Considerable sign has been passed, but we thought it best to let it alone as it is unlawful to trap in this [Indian reservation] country. After going 130 miles [actually about 70 miles] we entered Usher Canyon [Desolation Canyon].[12]

*September 18.* About 4 P.M. we saw some animals on the west side of the river. It was finally ascertained that they were what is called in this country "slow elk." These animals differ from other wild animals which are generally all of the same color. But slow elk are all colors of the rainbow. The one that fell victim to my

Lighthouse Rock, Desolation Canyon. The three boats of the second Powell expedition are tied up in the foreground. E. O. Beaman, 1871, U.S.G.S., Denver, Colorado.

rifle was white with speckles on the back, and in general appearance it strangely resembled a three-year-old steer.[13] Progress made: 20 miles.

*September 19–21.* The last two days were reserved to meat drying, and this morning [September 21] it was pronounced dry enough to move. Tonight we camp 20 miles deeper in the bowels of the earth. This canyon, so far, has been comparatively smooth, the rapids being short and clear. But the mountains, though not high, have been far more wonderful in their construction than any yet passed on the trip or, in fact, than any I have ever had the opportunity to witness. They are one continual string of gashes, sliced up and stood on edge. Domes piled on domes. There was one in particular we passed on entering the canyon, that stood alone, that was more the shape of a shot tower than anything else. It was perhaps 200 feet high, 40 feet at the base, 20 feet at the top, almost perfectly round, and to finish it up, a large flat rock was lying on the top. And, although there were hundreds of towers, steeples, spires, and many that represented the human head, and in fact representations of almost everything, the shot tower was far more wonderful than all the others. It was a thing to meditate on. How could it be put there so true in all its dimensions?

*September 22.* Last night we were awakened by a terrible rumbling noise. I sat up in bed and listened. The whole country seemed to be shaking, and my first thought was: earthquake! But after listening for a few seconds, it stopped with a terrible thud. It was only a portion of a mountain that had wearied of living in such a high altitude and had decided to take up a claim in the canyon below. After reaching its desired location it slept again and so did we.

This morning was very damp and had the appearance of becoming damper, and did. It not only rained, but in running a rapid that had a fall of about 10 feet in 130 yards, the rowlock jumped out. We came out at the bottom afloat as was everything else in the boat.

We camped early on account of rain. It was quite a romantic supper. No seats necessary, we stood under an old cottonwood tree without any limbs, holding meat and coffee in the same hand. When we wanted a bite of bread we would take it and then shove the piece back in our pocket to keep it from getting wet. We retired early as there were no places of amusement open. I had no desire to sleep, my arm pained me so, so I sat and listened to the gentle thunderstorm as it shook the mountains to their very base. There would be a clap of thunder and it would echo from cliff to cliff, back and forth 100 times. And when it would about die out, there would be another till it made one continual roar. Progress made: 22 miles.

*September 23.* The sun shone bright, but bright suns soon fade. After running five miles, the *Panthon* was turned bottom up on a bar per consequence of running a rapid that had one too many boulders in it. It is pretty hard to miss a boulder when you are within 10 feet of it before it is seen and going at the rate of 10 or 12 miles an hour, with a sea [waves] three or four feet high. It is all one man wants to do to keep her straight and not fall out himself. Well, there was a collision and the *Panthon* got her stem caved in slightly, but the carpenters had it repaired before evening.

The meat of the "elk" had got slightly damp after floating around in the boat for a half hour or so. It being cloudy, we decided to smoke it a little under a shelving rock that was about four feet high and 15 feet under. It was hung nicely back under and two fires were started (one on each side of it) and left to smoke while we repaired the boat. We forgot about it altogether. When we went back, it was all right, all cooked—broiled beef till you could not rest.

*September 24.* Good progress was made today. It has been the first day the sun has shone for a week. I think we had the winding-up shower last night, and it was one to leave an impression on memory. It was short, perhaps an hour. It started with a clap of thunder that seemed to split the Heavens open, and streaks of lightning that blinded me for quite a bit. Hail fell. The claps of thunder were terrible—it shook the boat like it was a feather. After it ceased, every side canyon was pouring its supply of water into the Green in a lively manner.

The steepest rapid of the trip was run today—23 feet in 400 yards [probably Three Fords Rapid at the head of Gray Canyon].

We saw a man just after dinner, coming toward us on a small flat that extended a short way in the interior, and he was coming as fast as his old gray could carry him. Thinking he wished to speak to us, we made a landing. He said he thought we had taken his boat. He was so excited he had not looked to see if his boat was gone. But he soon saw that our boat and the old box we had seen tied

In Gray Canyon near the mouth of Rattlesnake Creek. M. O. Leighton ca. 1910, U.S.G.S., Denver, Colorado.

up a mile or so above did not resemble each other in the least. We chatted with him a few minutes. He was the first man we had seen for 17 days. Progress made: 40 miles.

*September 25.* After an hour's run, Usher Canyon [Desolation and Gray Canyons], like the rest, was left in the rear. The last rapid [Swasey's Rapid] ran to the east causing the sun, which was about two hours high, to throw its rays right in my face. The rapid was all one glitter so nothing could be seen more than 10 feet ahead. But of course we paid no attention to such little things as that. The *Panthon* came out all right at the bottom, with two ribs cracked and one oar short.

At 12 A.M. I was at the post office in Green River, Utah,[14] and got our mail. We remained the balance of the day, most of it being spent in answering letters and letting our friends know that we still float. The people showed us great courtesy. Progress made: 17 miles.

34

# CHAPTER 2

# Green River, Utah, to Lee's Ferry, Arizona

*September 26.* I was a little sorry to leave so soon but, putting two more names on my new long list of correspondence, we pulled out early. We have supplied ourselves with provisions for six months. We drifted for two or three hours and in that time passed, without noticing, a very dangerous place in the river called "The Auger."[1] Everyone had told us to be very careful passing it, but we forgot. Probably we would never have thought of it again had not the people we next met mentioned it, and then I remembered. In the future, I am going to be a little more careful. Some of these times I expect we will get becked [thrown into a vat of liquid] and won't know anything about it.

We came to South Park Mining Company's plant. A placer mine, it resembled to some extent a wheat harvester at first sight. It is on trucks like a [railroad] car. In fact, it has car wheels under it and can be moved in any direction, notwithstanding its weight of 120 tons. It has a shovel that lifts one ton and a half. The machine has a capacity of handling 800 tons daily. Its motive power is electricity. Seven men (including the fireman and engineer) run the entire works. The powerhouse and works are about 300 yards apart but, of course, their distance varies. It is possible for them to be miles, as their connection is with wire. The plant, or rather the machine, cost $45,000.[2]

We stayed for dinner, and to make things more interesting we met Mr. John Hislop and W. H. [William Hiram] Edwards, two men that had been through the Grand Canyon with Stanton. They

View of Green River (City), Utah, and the Green River Valley, ca. 1910. M. O. Leighton, U.S.G.S., Denver, Colorado.

were expecting us and gave us a royal welcome, also lots of useful information. They said that we should call on a man at Lee's Ferry and get some life preservers they had left there, and also rubber bags.[3] Our road was long. Progress made: 22 miles.

*September 27.* The good-byes and good lucks were said, and the *Panthon* once more turned her prow south. Shortly after, a steamboat was passed. We did not go alongside for she was laid to rest far back on the land, far, far from her native water, for it was a steam launch (propeller) and was never intended for such waters as these.[4]

While drifting along in the afternoon, five mountain sheep were seen grazing up among the rocks. The sights of "Old Betsy" suddenly went up to 400 yards. The sheep ceased grazing. They probably thought the world had come to an end from the roar the 10 shots made that were sent in their direction. Two of them received fatal injuries. One, thinking it better to die in a higher altitude, started Heavenward among the rocks. The rest, being more bold, stood their ground, but before long they were stood on their heads. Not wishing to leave a poor dumb brute alone, wounded at that,

36

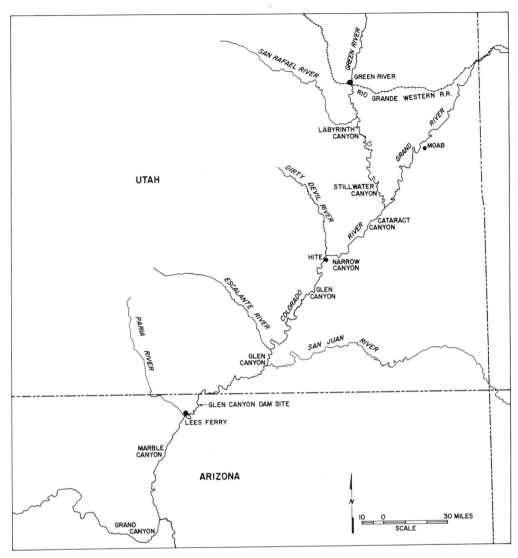

The canyon country of southeastern Utah, circa the 1890s.

we started on its trail (after taking the jackets off the other four) which led us up through gulches, over boulders, along the sides of walls where one slip of the foot would send us where we would never want any more sheep. After about an hour, climbing, sliding, and cussing, "Old 40" was discharged and the wounded sheep that had lived to see all the rest dead, gave a bound in the air and came

Trin-Alcove, Labyrinth Canyon. Here three side canyons enter the main canyon at the same point. E. O. Beaman, 1871, U.S.G.S., Denver, Colorado.

Bonita Bend, where Labyrinth Canyon ends and Stillwater Canyon begins. E. O. Beaman, 1871, U.S.G.S., Denver, Colorado.

down belly up. In a few moments the knife had played such havoc with it that it would have been hard to tell whether it had been shot or struck by lightning.

When we started campward, it dawned on us all of a sudden that it was just as hard to get down as up. But we arrived there just as the first rays of the moon were shedding their silver light on the scene. We both decided to take mutton for supper. Progress made: 17 miles.

*September 28–29.* We passed along through sluggish water, with nothing to be seen but the walls on either side, we having entered Still Water Canyon [Labyrinth Canyon][5] (100 miles long) so gradually we did not know it till suddenly we were aware we were walled in. Progress made: 60 miles.

*September 30.* At 2:20 P.M. we arrived at a place where a large creek came in from the east. There was a tent on the bank, but their boat was on the other side of the river. We knew they must be down the riverbank somewhere as the walls that set back a few yards defied scaling. I fired a shot as we passed the camp as a salute for the *Panthon* as she passed from the Green to the Red, for the

Junction of the Green (left) and Grand (center) rivers. E. C. LaRue, 1914, U.S.G.S., Denver, Colorado.

creek was the Grand River. Where the Grand and Green rivers meet they both lose their names, and there the great Colorado of the West starts on its wild and winding way to the sea.[6]

A couple of miles below the camp we saw smoke. I gave a loud call—it was answered by a shot. A landing was made with difficulty (the river having raised about 15 feet a few days before, and then lowered again, leaving the banks slippery and very steep at this point). The owners of the above mentioned camp were trying to smoke out a deer that had taken refuge in some brush. Introductions in these parts are of the short-order class. They came down to the boat and after an hour's fast talking it was time for the *Panthon* to move, for she could hear the roar of a rapid in the great Cataract Canyon.[7]

Looking downstream into Cataract Canyon, the first rapids visible in center of picture. E. C. LaRue, 1921, U.S.G.S., Denver, Colorado.

After making them a present of a leg of mutton, names were exchanged, hands were shook. They walked along the bluffs about a half mile so they could see us run the first rapid of Cataract Canyon. When they got at a point above, the *Panthon* soon showed the rapid a dry stern. But she got a wet head, and as we whirled out of sight (in only about a minute) we doffed hats once more with the two that stood on the cliffs, and shot out of sight and probably this world, to meet Mr. Summers and Mr. Gieger no more.

After running eight rapids in succession, we camped to let things dry out a little before night, for the rapids here are of a more extensive nature and I guess the sea (if such it can be called) will reach the height of seven or eight feet. This canyon seems to have a very bad name [reputation]. More than one boat and man have been called to their everlasting account here, but the *Panthon* must go through.[8] Progress made: 26 miles.

*October 1.* We started off rejoicing, running everything in sight. Every rapid would give us two or three buckets of spray which kept the bailing cup continually going. I was wet all the time, but as the weather is warm, no attention was paid to that.

Ramón said, "There is a deer!" I blazed away at it but missed. Three more put in an appearance. We made a landing and then they had more the appearance of antelope, and all fell just the same as if they had been. They were something I had never seen before. They were built on the same principle as a deer, but whiter and smaller. Their horns were about six inches long and flat like a goat's. The hams and saddles were put aboard.[9]

In a few moments we were at the head of another rapid. In running, or rather before running a rapid, we would go to shore, tie up the boat, and climb along the rocks and locate any boulders and see how the current ran. Then we knew just where to enter it. Sometimes, if possible, Ramón would climb down below the rapid and I would pick him up. He timed me in running two together and the time was 600 yards in 1/2 minute.[10] I would get above and in coming through shout, "Whoops! Aha!"

Well! The above mentioned rapid was pronounced runable. I put the *Panthon* in position and in she went. The sea came from both sides and knocked the oars out of the locks. I then lost control and went over a rock that was about two feet under the water. It caused a fall of about five feet, with a wave that combed upstream just below. The boat went over the rock all right, but dove her bow under the wave, scooping up enough water to fill her nearly half full. Well! I got out and to land. Everything was floating. There was a hasty transfer of everything to the shore, the things all being laid out on the rocks to dry. The sun very quietly stepped behind the mountains at 3 P.M. Progress made: 6 miles.

*October 2.* Today the drying continued. I found that the cataracts of the Colorado and the riffles of the Green were entirely different, and that our boat was too shallow and loaded too heavy to contend with waters that laid the boulders up in windrows, the same as a plow turns the furrow over. So while things were drying, I raised the sides, bow, and stern eight inches.

*October 3.* The work was completed about 10 A.M. and we pulled across to the other side to get in the shade. At 12 A.M. it was still

The rapids in Cataract Canyon are so numerous that most of them are simply numbered in downstream order rather than named. This is rapid number 44, now drowned out by Lake Powell. L. Lint, 1921, U.S.G.S., Denver, Colorado.

shady, though the canyon run about due south, so it can be imagined about how straight the walls are, or whether they lean over a little. Having our boat in better shape, her bow now being near three feet high, we were a little more seaworthy and made about 12 miles, running 18 rapids.

Ramón asked me if it was possible for a boat to turn a back summersault (he not knowing anything about a boat) for she would often stand in an almost perpendicular position. Just imagine a wave, say five feet high, standing still (for when they are made by the suction of a rock they don't move at all), and imagine running into it, at say 25 miles an hour. You go through pretty quick and I don't think it is an exaggeration to say that spray flies 10 feet high. Everything visible in the boat gets wet. Ramón sits aft and he gets his

43

pockets full of water from over the bow. I sit six feet farther forward than him—of course it is dry there!

*October 4.* Good headway was made today and just at camping time the walls fell from 3,000 to 1,000 feet which told us that the great roaring Cataract, with its 73 rapids (though 25 are not worthy of the name) was, like the Lodore, a thing of the past. Cataract Canyon is wonderful, with walls towering thousands of feet high. Ofttimes looking upstream, when four or five rapids were in sight, they bore a resemblance to steps, one above the other. I have had it in my mind that Cataract was the worst of all the canyons, but rope was only used once.[11] We only broke one rowlock, and got tangled up in only one rapid, and I am compelled to still give the honor to Lodore as being the worst. The only thing that is bothering me now is that two of those precious hams that were taken from those strange animals are about to spoil on our hands. The next creeping thing that comes to our sight will certainly be in danger. Progress made: 20 miles.

*October 5.* Narrow Canyon was before us. Being short, some 10 miles in length, this canyon was numbered with the dead before noon. Dirty Devil Creek was soon passed and we knew we were nearing Hite (or Dandy Crossing)[12] where we intended to send some letters out to let the world know we were still afloat.

About 2 P.M. something that bore a rude resemblance to a boat was seen tied to a rock. It, of course, called forth from my throat about two verses of a Commanche warhoop. It was answered in a minor key from behind a patch of willows, and out popped a man, very nimble and robust though his gray hair plainly told that his days were long on the land which the Lord thy God giveth thee. Of course conversation was swift. He had expected us to come for some days. We asked him how far it was to Hite. He told us we were in the city limits then, and within 100 yards of the post office. He was the postmaster, also the sole occupant of the town. We made camp and went over to the village, it being small, only a post office, hotel, and restaurant, all in a room 14×16 feet. The upper shelf of the cupboard was for letters; the mailbag hung on the bedpost. The house was built of round logs, and over the window a place about a foot long had been hewed so as to make a flat surface and in lead pencil was inscribed, "meals 35 cts."

Hite, Utah, now beneath Lake Powell. E. C. LaRue, 1915, U.S.G.S., Denver, Colorado.

We played high five [a card game] with him till it was time for the rooster to crow, and heard some of his history. He had dug for gold till his pick, patience, and soul were worn out, and at last, after 37 years (finding nothing), he had quit in disgust. He was passing his few last days brooding over the campfire, alone, thinking and picturing what he would have done if he had struck it rich. Progress made: 15 miles.

*October 6.* After taking breakfast with Mr. Wilson,[13] and grinding our ax and knives, we bade farewell to Hite and once more the *Panthon* turned her prow south.

*October 7–12.* We find ourselves at Lee's Ferry [Arizona] after seven days winding and twisting through Glen Canyon with its

Old placer mining equipment in Glen Canyon near Warm Spring Creek. E. C. LaRue, 1921, U.S.G.S., Denver, Colorado.

sluggish waters and barren peaks. This has been the most barren spot of our trip. Its walls are almost perpendicular the entire length, 155 miles, with a height of from 500 to 1,500 feet. The top, though level for a mountain, was destitute of vegetation or soil. It seemed as though the elements had took a pride in sweeping and washing it up to have at least one clean spot on the Colorado.

We passed three placer diggings that were in operation. The last place we stopped all night with them, and when we sat down to supper (as well as breakfast), I was not a little surprised when grace was said, thanking the Lord for the repast they were about to partake of (and so on). I thought it was kind of out of place when the meat on the table had been cruelly killed and carried off without the knowledge or consent of the owner. I know this to be a fact! (I gave them the meat.)

*October 13.* Well! We arrived here [Lee's Ferry] yesterday, and I went to the house which is some distance from the river. We were received by a billy goat, sheep, and hogs, but nothing that could talk. I skirmished around and my gentle voice echoed among the hills till it aroused four Navajo squaws up on a spur of the mountain, and they pointed down the river. I finally found out that the ferryman, postmaster, and sole occupant of the country was down below getting a boat the high water had deposited upon the side of the mountain. We built a large fire on the beach, which brought him up and, after a close inspection, it was found there were no letters for us. I was not a little surprised and finally came to the conclusion that our friends thought we were gobbled up in Cataract, and it would be no use to write to dead men. Well! If that should be the supposition, there will word go out of here to show they are mistaken![14]

It has been raining and the river is slowly raising. It is cloudy, but through the clouds and mist can be seen, faintly, the dim peaks of the Buckskin Mountains [Kaibab Plateau][15] which are a portion of the range which seems to choke the life out of the river, hemming it in and treading it down a mile and a quarter below their summits. But crowded, smothered, and squeezed as it was, it found its way to the sea, and tomorrow the *Panthon* will turn her head toward that great gash, 300 miles in length, where, like the river, may be throwed from rock to rock, spun round in whirlpools, and soon but in time, like the water, she will once more drift on quiet waters on toward the sea.

Tomorrow we start. Can a little flat-bottom boat ever go through such a place? The great Grand Canyon of not only the United States but the world? Can she live? Yes! Yes! What difference whether the walls be 100 feet or 100 miles? An eye that has had its vision blocked by mountains and deserts, and whose bed

The ferry at Lee's Ferry in operation in 1921. E. C. LaRue, U.S.G.S., Denver, Colorado.

has been the rocks or sand for years grows weary. What care they for high cliffs or deep gorges? Nothing! They travel in a kind of semi-conscious state, looking neither to the right or left. What care they for scenery? What care they for danger (when past)? What is there to live or die for? If the *Panthon* and her crew fail to put in an appearance at the other end, what difference will it make? None! She will go through without a doubt, but until she is through the doubt remains.[16]

*October 14–16.* Three days have passed and still we have not started. We decided it would be best to fix the boat up a little. Forty Navajo Indians passed here yesterday, headed for the Buckskin Mountains, and as our way lay through there I thought it would be best to load-up all the cartridges, for some of the former pages of this book will show that I have no (or ought to have) particular

48

regard, faith, or love for these good, civilized, harmless Indians, because they would not harm you in the least if they thought they would be found out. The first Indian I see skirmishing around my camp (out of civilization) goes to his everlasting account. Well! Tomorrow will find us in the regions of the unknown and if we should by accident or mismanagement stay, why farewell!

# CHAPTER 3

# The Grand Canyon

*October 17.* Ha ha! We are here! I don't know exactly where, but somewhere on top of a rapid [in Marble Canyon]. It is the second heavy rapid—Badger or Soap Creek. I don't know which is last and which is first, but the first [Badger Creek Rapid, mile 8] came very near being our last. We started out this morning singing, with two pairs of oars (having up to this time only had one) and the *Panthon* soon put 10 miles behind, when we came to a rapid that seemed to make considerable noise. After an investigation, we dove in, and came very near going a little too deep for our health. The bottom of the boat found a rock just in time to throw her sideways in the combing sea below. The shock was so hard, I had to drop the oars to catch myself from going overboard. I cast my eye to the lee gunwale—it was at the edge. I thought we were gone, but she raised and then I grabbed for the oars again. One had gone overboard, but with the remaining one I got her stem to the sea (it was not any too soon) and in a second we were winding and twisting around in the whirlpools below. It was all done in a flash. I don't suppose it was more than 20 seconds from the time we entered till we were out, so a person don't have much time to think. But after one is safe and thinks of it, they wonder how it was that the waves gave up when they had the power. It cannot be that water has mercy.

But we did not have long to meditate over our past danger. We found a pumpkin and that healed our wounds. It was not long till we heard the river groaning ahead which told of more work ahead,

Badger Creek Rapid, mile 8 (Badger Creek at right). Most of the rapids in the Grand Canyon are created by boulders which come bounding down steep side canyons during floods and then lodge in the less steep main channel of the Colorado. Raymond M. Turner, 1972, U.S.G.S., Tucson, Arizona.

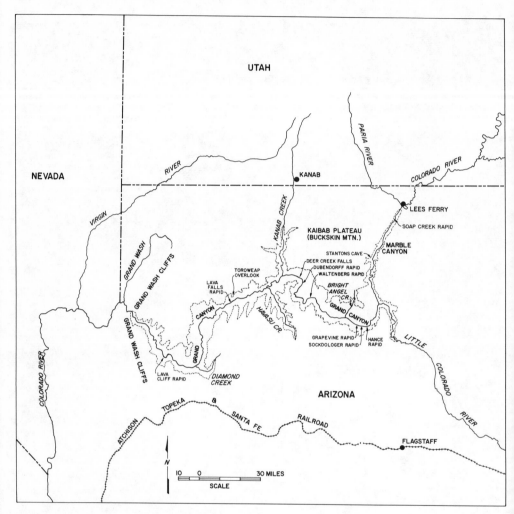

Northwestern Arizona, site of the Grand Canyon.

and soon we were tied up at the head of another rapid [Soap Creek Rapid, mile 11], crawling down over the boulders where we could get a good view. We viewed something to impress us for some time to come. It was some four or five hundred yards in length, the first 50 yards having about 12 feet of fall. It was rocky and seemed to be lashed into one mass of lather. We sat and gazed on it for two or three hours before our eyes had got their fill. The spray bounced 10 or 12 feet high, and as I was looking I noticed some 20 feet high, a dim mist of spray which puffed up like smoke. And it flashed

At the head of Soap Creek Rapid. George Wharton James, 1897, Arizona State Archives, Phoenix.

across my mind, "If you have any doubt where that smoke comes from, just try to run it!" Still, I could of run it with an empty boat, but it would have been too far to carry the stuff and it was decided best to make a portage. Everything was taken out of the boat, the tackles hooked on, and the boat was soon 10 feet above water. And though it was only 50 yards from the place of exit to entrance, it took half a day.[1]

After sliding her in the water again, we lowered her away 50 yards farther, behind a big boulder so as to break the waves, and got her sparred off and fixed up just in time to go to bed, which was pretty early. We were pretty tired, having a little more exercise than we were used to, such as carrying boxes, trunk, sacks of flour, beans, bacon, skinning our shins slipping over rocks, and other such little amusements. The inswell of the waves is making the *Panthon* dance, and we will be more than rocked to sleep tonight. The roar is so great it has made us dizzy. One side of the river seems

The Birdseye expedition of 1923 with a small boat much like the *Panthon*, lower part of Soap Creek Rapid, mile 11. E. C. Kolb, U.S.G.S., Denver, Colorado.

to be running one way, and the other, the other. Progress made: 12 miles.

*October 18.* It was 11:30 before we were ready to start, but once on the way lost time was made up for. During the afternoon 26 rapids were passed, seven very heavy ones.[2] One place Ramón was almost knocked overboard. The sea struck the boat so hard that the load was knocked from side to side. The river in one place was almost blocked with boulders [Boulder Narrows, mile 19]. Tonight we have marble slabs to sit on. Some of it is beautiful and there were brown, red, blue, yellow, and white in the same piece. Thought it seemed to be float, for there is no marble ledge visible above.[3] Progress made: 18 miles.

*October 19.* After going ahead for a short time, a ledge of white marble gradually rose up from the river and kept raising till both walls were one shining, glittering mass, probably 1,000 feet high. Then they ran back some distance, then up two or three thousand

54

Vasey's Paradise, Marble Canyon. Springs issue from the canyon wall at the left, the entrance to Stanton's Cave can be seen in the rock face at the right. Raymond M. Turner, 1983, U.S.G.S., Tucson, Arizona.

feet more. Several springs of clear water were passed, something new to us [Vasey's Paradise, mile 32]. Several caves were seen in the cliffs, but as the walls are too steep to climb, we only got to one. It ran in 100 feet and the top was covered with soot which showed someone had been there, but they were a more modern race than the Cliff Dwellers for a piece of rope was found there, something not used in those days, at least not grass rope.[4]

This part of the canyon is very abrupt and a shipwrecked sailor's eyes would water a long time before he could find a place to climb to the top of these walls. To stand on the summit and look down at the river (I doubt if it could be seen) must be an awful sight. It is far different looking up. After a thousand feet or so the top looks kind of dim, and if it was ten times as high it looks the same. There is marble enough here to build houses for the whole world

Junction of Little Colorado River (center) with the Colorado River. E. C. LaRue, 1923, U.S.G.S., Denver, Colorado.

to live in, and plenty to give them all a block to mark the spot where they take their last sleep. That little amount would not be missed from such a vast quantity.

This has been one of the most pleasant days we have passed. The rapids, probably feeling a little ashamed of treating us so rough, have been smoother than usual, and when we camped things were dry in the boat, something that had not happened for several days. We are down to dried beef and beans again, and the first animal that heaves in sight will be in immediate danger of being destroyed. Progress made: 25 miles.

*October 20.* When we started out we noticed the marble was raising and another formation was coming up underneath. It kept raising till it capped the highest peaks and later disappeared altogether. At 1 P.M. we reached the mouth of the Little Colorado River where we stopped and had dinner. This point [mile 61] is the terminus of Marble Canyon, and now the last, if not the least, is at hand, and when we pushed off with a rapid some 1/2 mile long to give us a good start, the *Panthon* shot into the great Grand Canyon at a lively rate and we camped with the Little Colorado far behind.

Marble Canyon was wonderful in its make up. It was a sight that made the heart shrink. To look up, it was truly awe inspiring! It made a man feel small. It showed him how small and insignificant he was. It made him not wonder, but *fear* and shrink before such mighty work! We saw nothing which gave us any reason to think that ever any such people as Cliff Dwellers had ever lived in the canyon. We saw a good many caves but nearly all were in perpendicular walls, and I have a doubt as to the Cliff Dweller story.[5] Progress made: 20 miles.

*October 21.* After going some 10 miles we came to a very bad rapid [Hance Rapid, mile 77]. Tying up the boat, we went down to investigate. It was one mass of boulders. The water entered by two channels at the head. It was perhaps as bad or worse (as for rocks) than any we had struck, and the show for running it was very slim, but to lower away would take at least a whole day.

While we were sitting there trying to decide what to do, we happened to look toward a little canyon that came in from the east side [Red Canyon], and to our surprise three mounted men came up, dismounted, and tied their horses. We were not over 50 yards apart. There was a hotel on top of the summit, a kind of summer resort, and they had come down from there.[6] They were much interested in the *Panthon*. One of these gentlemen was the Reverend Mr. George W. White, president of the University of Southern California at Los Angeles.[7] He had preached at the Methodist church at San Fernando and if I had attended church a little more regular, I might of known him. They were anxious to see us get over the rapid, and after having a long talk he gave me his card and requested me to write to him when we got through.

I decided to run the rapid (though I would not if they had not been there) and pushed off. We took the east entrance which was only a small portion of the river. We had to make exact points to get through, which we failed to do, and in the flash of an eye an oar was broke, a rowlock tore out, and the *Panthon* was piled up in the boulders. We were not yet in the main part. We took off our shoes and pants, and with the big end of the broken oar, I pried

Riders water their horses in the Colorado at the foot of New Hance Trail (at the head of Hance Rapid), mile 77 in the Grand Canyon, ca. 1906. Arizona Historical Society, Tucson.

her off. Twenty feet more and we came up again. Again we pried her loose. This time we whirled out in the main rapid. I took the head oars (the only ones left). She got across the current. Another rowlock busted—the oar went overboard—leaving no rowlocks on one side of the boat. There was only one narrow channel (crooked at that) where I thought it possible for a boat to pass, and we were hurled far from it. We went down sideways, endways, and every way, the three spectators standing on the rocks. I guess they would not of bid very high on what would be left of the *Panthon* and her crew when that rapid got through with them.

Well! Luck changes! Good follows bad. If we had bad luck in breaking the oar and rowlocks, we had good in getting through the rapid and we came out at the bottom never striking a rock. We picked up the oar that had followed up, and made shore just in time to keep from going over another rapid. Now, as I write these lines, I can look at the rapid that we came down not over 150 yards away. The rocks are as thick as seats in a theatre, and many are out of the water four feet. It seems impossible to think for a moment a boat could ever come through there in one piece. We made camp for the rest of the day and repaired the rowlocks and oars. Progress made: 10 miles.

*October 22.* This morning we were all ready again, but there was heavy water before us and before ten minutes had passed, we were again tied up to a rock, changing clothes, and bailing out the boat. We thought we had struck a rock slightly, but on investigation it was found that the bottom of the stem was cut off as clean as if with an ax, including a piece of iron which was also cut clean. Still, it did not damage the boat for the lost part was put there for a fender. In striking, it did not change the course of the boat in the least. At the time we were going about 15 miles an hour.

In a few moments we were off again, and in a few moments more we were again wet from head to foot, the boat about a third full of water, going down at 20 miles an hour. So much water had waterlogged her, she got sideways, but with will and strength I got head-on. This [Sockdolager Rapid, mile 79] was very long, some five or six hundred yards, and with a fall of at least 25 feet. Again the bailing began. Everything got wet again—the water in the boat was quite a way above shoe top. At the head of the rapid we ran over a sunken boulder, and as her bow went down between the next wave, some suction seemed to hold it down, some undercurrent, and the wave broke clear over. I never saw the like before.

It was no use to try to keep dry clothes, for any minute we were liable to be doused from head to foot (and were). There was no use to stop, so we pushed ahead. The rapids were thick! It seemed as though the boat was heavy—she would not raise quick and acted different than usual. She seemed stubborn and would not mind the oars.

It was 2 P.M. before we could find wood enough to make coffee. We, shortly after starting in the morning, had entered a box canyon. The walls came out of the water and were so straight that driftwood could not lodge. But at last, sighting a large stick that had jammed in a crevice, we had coffee and warmed ourselves for we were cold. It was cloudy and a fresh breeze coming down the canyon did not make wet clothes feel very comfortable.

After an hour we felt quite fresh again and off we went into another rapid. The spray flew—again we were bathed from head to foot, and so it was till we camped. It was nothing but bail and shiver all day. We ran somewhere in the vicinity of 40 rapids, and I think we had at least half that many barrels of water in the boat. Over half the time was spent in bailing, for it took 1/2 hour to bail out what came in in 1/2 second.

One place the rapid filled from wall to wall and there was not the least footing anywhere [Grapevine Rapid, mile 82]. It was about 1/2 mile long and straight and I think had a 30 foot fall. At the lower end the spray was flying high—it looked hazy! It was very risky to run it, knowing not what was at the bottom. To try to lower away would probably take two or three days. To avoid that much work by one single minute's risk was tempting (though that one minute is enough to smash the boat into a thousand pieces and put ourselves in a destitute condition if not in eternity). We were tempted; and a minute later we were past and once more the gauntlet was run. But this kind of water cannot last long. We are taking up too much fall and, to make a rough guess, I should think we are between three and four hundred feet lower than when we started this morning.

We dried ourselves out and after supper we talked over the day's proceedings. It was decided by the majority as being the most dangerous, as well as the luckiest, day of the whole trip. Lucky to think we are afloat tonight. If we had lowered over all the bad places it would have taken a month, and by risk it was run in a day. Still, I feel confident we will get through. We must expect some accidents and expect to hit some rocks. There is only one stone we must not hit, that we must miss at all hazard—our tombstone! Progress made: 17 miles.

Looking upstream to Grapevine Rapid, mile 82. Canyon walls that come down right to the water's edge make a portage impossible. L. R. Freeman, 1923, U.S.G.S., Denver, Colorado.

still; g feel confidence we will get through! we must
expect some accidents! and expect to hit some rocks
there is only one stone! we must not hit! that! we must
miss at all hazzard! (our Tomb Stone!)
after Breakfast the cargo was all hung out to dry for
the third time, and for the fourth time, the
Penthon was hauled up for Repairs the few ragged
pieces left on her Bow were torn off, and in a short
time, she had a new Bow. as it needed a piece of
iron. it was necessary to procure it from some
source, so a steel Frh. fell victim. it was heat
in the fire. to bend it in the right shape,
(a pair of scissors, were used as tongs) it fit
to a tee, she was once more pushed back into
the river, and later on loaded up where she
swang to the Painter, like a gentle horse, scarcely drawing it tight, and ready to dare the waters
tomorrow. let them be smooth! or rough! but
rough though they be, they will only get a chance
to dash against her side as she passes, to the
greats like the small! are all the same. they are
seen ahead, they are seen at hand, and at last
left far behind rock once passed! are harmless,
those that are far ahead, can harm us not. we only
water. those close under the Bow that lays low in
the water. to strick like a murderer in tin s.....g
the next day was not without its accidents, we had
not gone f., before we were wet to the skin, and as usual
Bailing occupied most of the time, we got in a whirlpool. that took complete charge of everything, it spun
us around for several minutes, and then hurled us
against the rocks, taking us back again, whirling
us around for another small E. turning it threw us
in a little cove, about 30 ft square. every time we
tried to get out we were sent back, after trying
this a few times. to no avail. we stoped to figure
out some way of escape. we watched the worlpool

23,495

A page from Flavell's logbook.

*October 23.* After breakfast the cargo was all hung out to dry for the third time, and for the fourth time the *Panthon* was hauled up for repairs. The few scattering pieces left on her bow were torn off and in a short time she had a new bow. As it needed a piece of iron, it was necessary to procure it from some source, so a steel trap fell victim. It was heated in the fire to bend it in the right shape (a pair of scissors were used as tongs). It fit to a tee. She was once more pushed back into the river (and later on loaded up) where she swung to the pointer like a gentle horse, scarcely drawing the line tight and ready to dare the water tomorrow. Let them be smooth or rough, but rough though they be, they will only get a chance to dash against her side as she passes, for the great, like the small, are all the same—they are seen at hand, and at last left far behind. Rocks once passed are harmless. Those that are far ahead can harm us not. We only watch those close under the bow, that lay low in the water to stick, like a murderer, in the back.

*October 24.* Today was not without its accidents. We had not gone far before we were wet to the skin and, as usual, bailing occupied most of the time. We got in a whirlpool that took complete charge of everything. It spun us around for several minutes and then hurled us against the rocks. Taking us back again, whirling us around for another small eternity, it threw us in a little cove about 30 feet square. Every time we tried to get out we were sent back. After trying this a few times to no avail, we stopped to figure out some way of escape. We watched the whirlpool and noticed it was not always the same. It boiled with a great force, then it calmed a little for a new start. We got everything all ready and when it lulled we shot out. It was too quick for us and back we went against the rocks again. After four or five trials we got out.

After 5 P.M. we ran a heavy rapid [probably Waltenberg Rapid, mile 112]. Though smooth in the middle, it was very rough at both top and bottom. It did not look very bad so in we went. The first dash filled the boat half full. I thought we were going to fill, for the next dash was as bad if not worse. I kept her head-on and as level as possible. She went through. As usual, when we have bad luck with a rapid there is always another just at its foot, but our luck was in and we made the shore about 20 feet above it [112.5 Mile Rapid].

Needless to say things in the boat were somewhat damp. Camp was soon made. We had collided with several rocks during the day and we find, for the first time, the boat to be leaking a little. The country is changing somewhat. For the last 25 miles the canyon has been very narrow. The walls, though not very high (1,000 feet) were stood on their edge, the strata stood straight up and down, and all kinds of formations mixed together till they resembled a bookcase with all kinds of different colored books standing side by side. But in the afternoon the hills broke down and showed a little verdure in places. The high mountains have receded so far back they are shut out from view by the smaller ones that still hem the river.

We find the water the most pleasant in deep box canyons. When we get into broken country where the sun can get in, it seems to make the water playful and it tries to see how high it can jump. But so far the *Panthon* has been equal to the occasion. When we get knocked around so that we can't manage her, she hunts her own way through, tapping a rock now and then just to see if it is solid. Progress made: 20 miles.

*October 25.* This morning the sun came in to see us at 9:30. The rapids took a change—instead of trying to swamp us (as was their usual habit) they shot us ahead at a lively rate, now and then playfully sprinkling us a little.

At 1 P.M. we stopped to have lunch. While eating, a large buck ibex [bighorn sheep] came down the mountain to see what the smoke meant. After coming to within 300 yards, he stopped. I expected to see him go back a-flying. We needed meat, and a random shot was better than none. Taking a rest against a rock, the ball passed over his back, but the next broke a leg. Then there was a race up the mountain till the foot of the main wall was reached, then along the wall, over canyons, gulches, ravines. But he refused to give us his hide and I was forced to come back without meat.[8]

We traveled on. At 4 P.M. heavy rapids were encountered again, but they were soon passed [probably Specter and Bedrock rapids, mile 129–130]. In one I think the boat dropped 10 feet in a hole made by a sunken boulder, but she raised on the next wave which lifted us high in the air and we came out dry.

At 5 P.M. we came to a very bad rapid, full of rocks [probably Deubendorff Rapid, mile 132]. To try to run the main channel was

A boatman of the Birdseye expedition battles Waltenberg Rapid, mile 112. L. R. Freeman, 1923, U.S.G.S., Denver, Colorado.

sure destruction, but it was possible to run the inside of the curve. It was also full of rocks and shallow, but we thought we would run it anyway. If we hung up we would pry off, and going through that way was better than lowering. In we went. We missed the

Deer Creek Falls, mile 136 in the Grand Canyon. E. C. LaRue, 1923, U.S.G.S., Denver, Colorado.

exact place to enter. She struck once, turned clear around, and came out flying, but that blow was harder than we had expected.

We made a landing on the bar below and found the side was mashed in, including the piece of iron. This was the first time the boat had been actually damaged—it called for a sudden discharge of cargo. The bow was pulled up on the rocks so the damaged part was above water. The splinters were cut away, and pieces fitted on the inside, nailed and caulked. Progress made: 16 miles.

*October 26.* At 10 A.M. this morning she was ready to proceed. We passed through a dark, or rather black, formation that shone like coal, though it was not. It was about 60 feet high and about two miles long, and it lacked about one degree of being perpendicular. The channel for the river was narrowed to 60 feet [actually 76 feet] in the narrowest place and not over 80 in the widest, this being the narrowest cut so far on the river [Granite Narrows, mile 135]. As we drifted along we noticed the lower walls were sinking and the second bench was closing in; and at 1 P.M. we were encased in walls thousands of feet high, perhaps a mile or more, lacking only a degree or so of being perpendicular. The east side had three benches, the first 600 to 1,000 feet being mostly of marble of a dark soapstone color. From the top of the first bench it was two or three hundred yards back at the angle of 45° to the foot of the second, then an abrupt wall of 2,000 feet more, the third bench being the same way. It was wonderful to look up (being necessary to look twice to see the top). The tops looked dim. The few scattering pines on their summit looked like small blades of grass. The river being so crooked, it could only be seen for a few hundred yards each way, and made it appear as though we were in a great deep pit.

This had been another fine day and we shot along at five miles an hour. Only six bad rapids were encountered, but these were run without getting wet. A falls was passed about noon that fell from the west wall [Deer Creek Falls, mile 136]. It was small, being a stream four feet wide and a foot thick. It had a fall of about 400 feet.

Later in the day an old doe and fawn ibex were seen on the first bench. A landing was made and after hunting along the wall for 1/2 mile, I found a crevice and, with a few minutes of hard climbing, I gained the bench, but no ibex in sight. I climbed to the foot of the second bench and followed around the rim for a mile or so, but was forced to go back to camp and eat *carne seca* [dried

View looking downstream into the inner gorge of the Grand Canyon from Toroweap Overlook, mile 177. J. K. Hillers, 1872, U.S.G.S., Denver, Colorado.

meat] for supper. The foot of the second bench gave an extensive view of the river. It looked very small from a perch of nearly 3,000 feet, and the cliff above seemed to be just as high above as when I was at the water's edge 3,000 feet lower. The wind, toward dark, began to come up the canyon with a vengeance which seemed to indicate a storm. Progress made: 25 miles.

*October 27.* This morning it was very dark (not being any too light at the best of times). The weather looked bad. Preparations were made to start, but a few large drops of rain warned us to keep covered up. The drops kept increasing till they fell in torrents, and I fear there will be a raise of the river. If such be the case we will have to lay up till it goes down. I am not much stuck on storms in such a place as this, for every rain loosens rocks above which come plunging down to the river as though they wanted to knock it out of existence. No thanks! I don't wish any 10 or 20 thousand ton boulders flying around my ears!

At 2 P.M. it cleared up a little. Camp was broke and though it sprinkled some again, we kept going and did not stop till the shadows of night had drawn their curtain over the canyon. Progress made: 15 miles.

*October 28.* This morning it was cold. At 9 A.M. the *Panthon* was moving. A bad rapid [Lava Falls Rapid, mile 179] was run which put about eight inches of water in the boat.[9] It was pretty fresh, but we had to stand it. The north wall (for the river runs west the entire length of this canyon) commenced to show indications of having been warmer some day than it is at present. It had been boiled up, the lava had run down the side in streams, in some places it had run down canyons, cooling before it reached the bottom, making quite a contrast between the light colored sandstone and the black lava. And though it lasted for many miles, it seemed as though the great river had even dared to face a burning volcano and did not allow it to cross, for only now and then a small knob or bed could be seen on the south side and seemed to be thrown across. The appearance of the rock shows the volcano was not in action long, for the rock was not burnt to any great extent, and in my estimation it was just an upheaval.

Early in the morning we saw some little streams coming down from a bench about 20 feet above the river, and on investigation we found there was a *ciénega* [marsh] of five or six acres. On the edge we saw what seemed to be the skeleton of some beast, but on closer examination it was found to be petrified tules, reeds, rushes, and other kinds of grass. The ground seemed to have been heated up from underneath, heating everything to what seemed to be a melting heat, and then cooling, turning everything to stone. The earth seemed to be consumed and in many places there were cavities three or four feet deep, the roots hanging there like icicles, all hard as stone. In walking around it was like walking on clay pipes as they cracked and snapped underfoot. Picking up a few pieces, we moved on.[10]

Seeing a shack on a bar, we landed again and found eight teepees or wigwams which showed the red man had been there (but was gone then).[11] We saw moccasin tracks at another place and other evidence of the red man.

It was 12 A.M. before the sun got down to see us. The river running west as it does, and the sun so far south, it cannot get down over such barricades as these walls and we have not had, on an average, one hour a day of sunshine since we left Lee's Ferry. But after 1 P.M. the walls on the south broke down and continued to do so all the afternoon. The river took a turn south and tonight the sun set on the west side for the first time in many days. At 4 P.M. the river, seeming (like ourselves) tired of being hemmed in, shot ahead, anxious to get out of the canyon (for the end is now near) and carried us along at seven miles an hour. Progress made: 40 miles.

*October 29.* This morning the sun came in at 8 o'clock, the east walls having broken down completely, leaving only a rugged, broken, chopped up country. But before many miles were passed, a new set of walls (granite) slowly arose out of the river and again we were walled in. But the river now commenced to run in all directions, giving the sun a chance every now and then to glance up-and-down the canyon.

After our 2-1/2 days of pleasant sailing, bad water was encountered. The rapids were numerous, crooked, and rocky. We were getting reckless, so much so we drew no line. We ran 13 heavy and very dangerous ones. After running everything so far in Grand Canyon, we will now take very desperate chances for, if our calculations are right, this is our last night in the Canyon.

The next to the last rapid we ran this afternoon was as dangerous as any on the whole river [Lava Cliff Rapid, mile 246].[12] There was a large boulder in the middle of the river the size of a small house where most of the water piled up and broke off on both sides. To the right it was filled with smaller rocks—it was impossible to pass that side. There was a pass of 30 feet between the rock and the left side, which was a high perpendicular wall that curved around behind the rock, so the water, after breaking off the rock, went to the wall. Where the water runs to the wall is a very bad place, for if the boat once touches she is gone. But we thought by cutting close to the rock we could shoot around behind. We went in, and having to pull quite a little to clear the rock (which was just as dangerous as the wall if struck), we pulled too far. I thought we were gone. I threw her around, head-on, to let her strike bow first. But just as her bow was within four or five feet of the wall, there

View looking upstream from Toroweap Overlook, mile 177, 1962. Arizona Historical Society, Tucson.

Paiute wickiups on the North Rim of the Grand Canyon. J. K. Hillers, 1872, Arizona Historical Society, Tucson

72

was a boil-up—it stopped the headway of the boat, or rather gave her a kind of a push out (though we still were going 20 miles an hour) and in a second we were past, missing the point by less than two feet. That was the nearest call we have had and we consider ourselves under many obligations to that little boil-up, it being the only thing in the world that could have helped us.

The walls being so abrupt, we went till dark before we could find wood enough to make a fire. Well! Twenty-five miles more and the great Buckskin Mountains will be lost to view. Only 25 short miles. That is only a very short distance compared with the hundreds already passed, but still it is 25 miles and it must be passed before we can say our life is our own. But tomorrow night we will be safe on the lower Colorado, wrecked, or dead. Which will it be? Progress made: 35 miles.

*October 30.* Having an early start and desiring to have it over, the oars were bent, stopping only a few minutes for dinner. The rapids came regular, but one by one their waves were mashed down by the *Panthon*'s bow. The walls kept raising up and breaking down, only to raise again. Still, the same steady stroke was kept, and at 3:20 P.M. the walls stopped to raise no more.[13] We looked ahead at the low, rolling hills and the river which spread wide, with groves of willows on both banks. We looked back at the high and rugged peaks now left behind. We were safe, a feeling no one could feel while in that terrible place! But now the Great, Grand, Beautiful, Wonderful, Fearful, Desolate Canyon is like yesterday—passed!

It is an awful place, and destitute to the extreme. In all its barren walls there is not a single bat's nest—not even they would live in such a desolate place.[14] Language can convey only a faint idea of such a place, for the literature put before the public is so different in its description from the real canyon, it would not be recognized. I have a handy manual which says the walls are 7,000 feet perpendicular. There is no place on the Colorado River where there is a perpendicular wall raising out of the river that will exceed 3,000 feet. It appears more as though the river ran between two ranges instead of one. The highest peaks are seldom seen from the river, for they are far back (as a general thing) and the inner walls shut them out from view. And ofttimes when the walls are only a few hundred feet high, nothing can be seen beyond their tops, the higher peaks being so far back. Still, there are times when high peaks come close, but always in benches—four, five, or six, sometimes more. At the top of each bench it takes a slant back from a few feet to 1/2 mile which sets the summits far back. The most extensive formations are sandstone, granite, and marble. Streaks of marble can be found at the canyon's mouth.

I don't think there is another such barren country in the world as the one we have passed through (unless it is the Sahara). Over a thousand miles, it is (properly speaking) one entire canyon from beginning to end. In all that long distance there is not one foot that can be called level land with the exception of 2,000 acres at Blake [Green River, Utah]. There are in Utah a good many little bottoms and bars containing a few acres each, but it is a poor foundation to build on, for they were made by the river and are subject to transportation at any high water. In all that distance only fourteen deer, seven sheep, seven ibex, two jackrabbits, and two flocks of quail were seen. For the last 700 miles there are not enough beaver to count. Where we expected to find many we found none, and all we made from such a long and dangerous trip was our escape! Still it is worth half of a life (such as I lead) to see such a place.

When I come to explain what was there, language fails. When a person speaks of going at a 20 mile rate and a five mile an hour current, it might lead people to think that a boat ought to go a long way in a day. Twenty mile currents don't go far at a time. We will take a rapid, for instance 300 yards long, with a 20 foot fall, that will propel a boat 20 miles an hour by the time she reaches the bottom. Now, starting in such a rapid (they are all the same in proportion) the water is smooth at the top, but as the water gains speed, the waves form, always coming to a funnel shape at the bottom. As soon as the bottom is reached, whirlpools form on each side. Still, the rapid rushes on in the center for a hundred yards or so, getting smaller and smaller till it is lost altogether, and then everything is one foaming, boiling, sucking mass. It is just as liable to take the boat upstream as any direction. Sometimes a boil may set you out at the bottom of the bench, and though the water 10 feet from the boat is going downstream it is impossible to get in the current, the boil keeping the boat boiled back in the eddy. The best way is to just take a rest till the whorls and eddies get tired of spinning the boat—then they take her out themselves.

We have passed 779 rapids on our journey, 269 being on Green River. There is one in Lodore Canyon, which no boat could ever

oking across the head of Lava Cliff Rapid, mile 246. This rapid is now drowned out by Lake Mead.
R. Freeman, 1923, U.S.G.S., Denver, Colorado.

pass, the river running under a shelf [Lower Disaster Falls].[15] But with that exception, there is always a chance, though we considered it best to use rope six times during our trip: four times in Lodore, once in Cataract, once in Marble, though we afterward ran places far worse (excepting the one in Lodore Canyon).

We did not count the rapids of the Marble and Grand canyons as their number was already known, but we kept count of the worst ones, which numbered 130. In running those there is equal chance, one for one, and we won every time! Often after investigating a rapid, I went back to the boat with a vague uncertainty as to which side would be up when we got through. Still, my mind was made up to run it before it was seen. It was only investigated to find the best side to take. If it curved, or if it looked dark, or if the foam was flying, it was all the same—run it anyway! If we could run one, we could run another. Recklessness grows, and if the last rapid had been as bad as that below the Niagara, we would have went in and trusted to luck. There is a great many stories told of the falls (perpendicular) and of the river running downhill, but I can say that there is no place where the river has a fall of over 15 feet to 100 yards, or a place where it has over 50 feet of fall to any one mile. I don't think there is any single rapid that has over a 35 foot fall—still that is pretty steep.[16] Progress made: 40 miles.

# CHAPTER 4

# The Lower Colorado River

*October 31.* We had not gone but a few miles when fresh sign was seen. Camp was made. We can't afford to pass any beaver now and we shall trap every track from here on. We have still 500 miles before us, but the river is smooth. Although there are canyons ahead, there is only one rapid of any consequence, called the Walapai [in Virgin Canyon, 25 miles downstream from Grand Wash Cliffs], but I have run that before in a boat not half so good as the *Panthon*, though it is pretty heavy. Having such poor luck [trapping] above and getting through so soon leaves a long winter before us and I think the *Panthon* will dive her bow into the salt water before the trip is ended, for beaver are few and Yuma will soon heave in sight.

*November 1 to December 23.* In a few days we arrived at Temple Bar mining camp where I met several old friends.[1] We tied up, as there was no need of rushing now. I built them a boat, and it was a month before we again moved.

We next came to the Virgin River.[2] The people living there were glad to see me, we having known each other for years. After staying one night we again passed on, picking up a beaver here and there, stopping at mining camps, for having trapped the river so long, everyone knows me and to pass without stopping would never be forgiven.

We soon passed all the camps, Fort Mohave being the only place we did not stop. After passing there we soon arrived at Needles[3]

Temple Butte, Clark County, Nevada. L. R. Freeman, 1923, U.S.G.S., Denver, Colorado.

Looking downstream on the Colorado toward The Needles, ca. 1905. The river has a broad floodplain covered with cottonwood, willow, and other water-loving plants that in Flavell's day provided excellent beaver habitat. Bancroft Library, University of California, Berkeley.

and got the mail, some of it having been to Lee's Ferry. I remained only a couple of days. Ramón quit the ship at this point, so I was compelled to finish the journey alone, but I was used to that. Again I sallied forth, and one after one the days passed, and one after one the beaver skins piled up in the boat.

*December 24.* I arrived at the Mohave Agency and Indian School.[4] I went up, or rather back, about 1/2 mile where it was situated, and asked for mail. I asked for Flavell. There being none, I then asked for Clark. They had all heard of Clark, in fact there was a man in the house I was well acquainted with. He had passed down the river a couple of days before and had told them about me. He knew me by Clark, and when I asked for Clark they wanted to know if he was not coming up. I told them I was that man I guessed. Out popped Jennings from another room and a hasty introduction took place. I went back to the boat shortly after.

They wanted to see the boat that had shot the Grand Canyon, and soon I had visitors aboard of both sex, and it was decided I

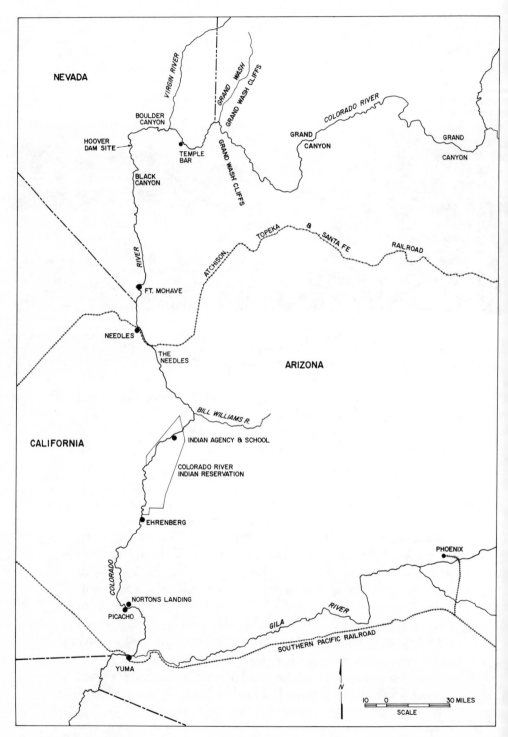

The lower Colorado River.

Colorado River near mouth of Bill Williams River, Arizona. George Wharton James, 1898, Southwest Museum, Highland Park, Los Angeles, California.

should stay over Christmas. So after the firestorm of questions were answered, they went back to finish the Christmas tree, and I made a few changes, hastily, and again put in an appearance.

About sundown, or a little before, I went out to a building where they were issuing out stuff to the old Indians. The whole community had assembled, humanity in all stages. Some were crippled, some were blind, some were a week old, and some were more than a hundred years. Of course in issuing out things some got left, that is got nothing, and after it was closed, one, or rather many, who got nothing grumbled. One old squaw, perhaps 70 or 80 years of age, came out in front with a large stick in her hand. She went through a long sermon, at the same time making gestures with the stick as though it was a spear. She talked about two minutes, then, perhaps thinking she was throwing her words away (as no one understood), she gave a genuine old warhoop and walked away. We adjourned, or they did. The old bucks and squaws went back to their huts, the children back to their quarters (they had been allowed a holiday during Christmas week).

After supper I was conducted to the hall where the Christmas tree was (the first I had seen for 16 years). After things were all ready, the children were marched in. The first was a girl of perhaps 16 years. They got smaller as the line passed, and the smallest were perhaps six years of age. Then came the boys, about the same in age, also in number. The girls were dressed in dark blue with three white stripes around the waist and wrist. All wore shoes of the toothpick pattern, and the dresses of the largest girls were provided with bloomer sleeves. The boys were also clad in dark blue, brass buttons, and caps with patent leather beaks. After they were all seated they sang a song of Christmas. Some spoke pieces. Later on Santa Claus was heard making a racket in the chimney that had been erected, and out he tumbled. Every child got a pair of stockings containing candy, oranges, etc. There was something for everybody, no one was missed. Santa Claus having finished his work retired to the chimney, and the children to bed.

The faint sound of a violin could be heard in another building. I mosied in that direction with the rest. Shortly after our arrival the violin struck a higher key and someone said, "Get your partners for a quadrille!" and in less than the twinkle of an eye, I was swinging. The cook, the chaplain, superintendent, teachers, matrons were all mixed up. No one knew who was who and no one cared. Everybody tried to make everybody else happy. I forgot all about the Colorado River and Grand Canyon till the clock held both hands up in amazement. Good night passed from lip to lip and all retired to their respective quarters while I, against the will of all, sought my way through the brush to the bank of the river where my boat was tied. I tumbled in to meditate on the life I lead and the one I might lead.

*December 25.* It was 10 A.M. before I arose from my virtuous couch of sheepskins, and after taking coffee I again pushed through the brush. After dinner I passed the evening playing croquet. When the bell rung for the children's supper I went in with the superintendent. They all marched as on the night before, girls first. I took a seat, and after supper was over the line went out again. The tables were cleared by the girls, and then I received a surprise. Indian children, as a general thing, are very reserved and it is hard to get

Mohave Indian girls, ca. 1900. Arizona Historical Society, Tucson.

rung for the Childrens supper, I went in
with the Superentendant, they all marched
as on the night before, Girls first to I took a
seat, and after super was over, the line went
out again. the tables were cleared by the girls
and then, I recieved a supprise. indian children
as a general thing very reserve. and it is
hard to get a word out of them. and you may
imagine my supprise. when the line broke
the smallest girls from 6 to 10. came running
to me, and got all around, they all wanted
to know my name, and they told what each
others names were (they all have English
names rangeing from Lucy Gray, to Red
riding Hood,) I was supprised to hear them
talk English so well. when I told them my
name, I could hear them spelling it all
around me. they asked me where my home
was. and when I told them, I had none, they
could not understand that, and they asked
several times. feaing, perhaps I did not
understand. when I go out side, the Boys
all had the same questons to ask. and the
answer No Home! puzzled them too. later
on, they were all called into the sermon room
and from their to bed. with the exception
of not the largest Girls. which were brought
to the dance as it was to be arranged for
two set to dance at a time. but there wa
a mistake some way, and only 3 got to dance
well! next morning at ten I was forced to push
off from the bank once more, I had said Good
by, to all about midnight. the Doctor a young man.
being the last. He walked a ways with me. 2 hours
later, found me in his office, He was trying to
perswade me to not pass. Yuma. not to cross
the Mexican lines, his words had considerable

a word out of them, and you may imagine my surprise when the line broke—the smallest girls first, from six to ten, came running to me and got all around. They all wanted to know my name and they told what each other's names were (they all have English names ranging from Lucy Gray to Red Riding Hood). I was surprised to hear them talk English so well. When I told them my name I could hear them spelling it all around me. They asked me where my home was, and when I told them I had none, they could not understand that and they asked several times fearing, perhaps, I did not understand. When I got outside, the boys all had the same questions to ask, and the answer, "No home," puzzled them too. Later on they were all called into the schoolroom, and from there to bed, with the exception of eight of the largest girls, which were brought to the dance as it was to be arranged for two sets to dance at a time. But there was a mistake some way and only three got to dance.

*December 26.* Well! This morning at 10 I was forced to push off from the bank once more. I had said good-bye to all about midnight, the doctor, a young man, being the last. He walked a ways with me. Two hours later found me in his office. He was trying to persuade me to not pass Yuma, not to cross the Mexican line. His words had considerable effect. He seemed to think more of me than I did of myself. He said it would show more true honor to stay away and hold them in contempt than it would to try to seek something I could never gain, and if I went, it would actually lower me in their estimation. Still, that brings me no comfort. Well! When I pushed off, the team was standing on the bank—several had come down to see me off. I was soon out of sight.

When I made camp tonight, to say I was lonesome would be putting it very light, and when an Indian that had smelled the campfire put in an appearance, he was welcome indeed. If all Indian schools are conducted in the same manner as the one I have just spoken of, I shall be compelled to change my view somewhat. It is said that the Yuma Indian School, or rather the children that go there, all follow the same occupation after leaving school (bar the boys). I have seen them hundreds of times. I never could get one word of English out of them. But the children at the place I have just left like to talk English. The little girls are very kind and affectionate which shows they have been treated with kindness, and a government that takes such interest in children should be showed some clemency, and I guess I will have to stand by her.

Still, for well I know, if one of those children were murdered by a white man, he would be run to earth and hung. But if an American or two happens to cross the [Mexican] line and accidently get shot full of holes and eaten up by people [Seri Indians] who carry official documents which show the government permits, or rather does not object to, their dining on an American or two now and then, of course the poor Indian don't know any better. But if the Mexican Government don't know any better either, it should be the one to pay. If they want to harbour such people, they should be made to pay for their depredations.

Still, some may say, and have said, we had no business to go there. I know that myself now! But if it had not been for Mr. Francisco Aguilár, who was prefect of Hermosillo at one time, and who appointed a governor of Tiburon Island at the same time, furnishing him with documents to show that he was recognized by the Mexican authorities and all who came would have to recognize him also (I did and would if I should have the pleasure of seeing him again). If it had not been for that piece of handiwork of Mr. Francisco Aguilár, our crew would not have been so short on leaving. Of course, at that time there was a doubt as to it being true. There is no doubt now! And also at that time there was trouble at home and every effort was necessary to stop the great strike which was then at hand. There is no strike, no doubt, now.[5]

Then there is another great drawback—the old saying, "Everyone can be judged by the company they keep." Rich governments must associate with rich people. If a rich man went down there and was killed, the country would be in arms in 24 hours, if there was money enough behind it. But it could not disgrace itself by stooping to help the poor. But if there was a war and I did not go, I would be disgraced. Yes, they would expect me to grab a musket and shed the last drop of blood I had to save the country, whooping "Freedom or Death" in my ear, and so on. But if I was burnt at the stake it would be quite a different thing, and perhaps I was as close as ever a man was and escape. Still there is a cry for help ringing in my ears from men that were indirectly slaughtered by the Mexican Government. And it has been said, if ever I am caught across the line, I will be made to repent. And for what? Telling the freight wagons and hauled to Prescot Phoenix Tuscon San Bernardino and other parts. then Ehrenburg flourished and had a population of over 2000 now! Presect Phoenix and all those places have Rail Roads. the ships have stoped comaing to the River. there was no freight to haul. the teams were driven to other parts. sold or left to a lingering death by starvation. the People dissapeared one. by one and to day Ehrenburg is fighting hard. to keep its name off of the Deatha Record. in front of the Houses. where once children played. lies the remains of Leavt Wagons a Hub. here and a Tire there still! the inhabitants are not all gone there is still a store run by Mr Thomas Hamillton He is Post Master. Justice of the Piece. runs a Black smith Shop. and a Ferry Boat. after passing one night I passed on The next 100 miles was not inhabited but every now and then the old wall of a house could be seen on a Mesa or Table land. which showed some one had mistaken dross for Gold and after finding his mistake had packed his Buros again to explore other regons leaveing. His house to return no more there it stands. like a Tomb and will still stand for they are all made of Earth and Earth can not decay later on. Nortons Landing was passed. it is also on the verge of the Grave Picacho still lives. I passed there at sundown and twelve next day tied Up at Yuma a poorer but Wiser man the trip is endd 1685. miles of passing scenery. Gone I am now ready for a other trip but before I go farther south I guess I had botte hesitate a moment at least

Jin 8th 97    The End    George F Flavell

Ehrenberg, Arizona, in its heyday in the late 1800s. Arizona Historical Society, Tucson.

truth! I have been told, to cross the line is equal to signing my death sentence. Still, I have got a damn good notion to get...

*December 27 to January 8, 1897.* Two or three days after writing the above, the north wind was howling. I was camped in a nice sheltered place. I saw someone coming up the other side of the river, poling a boat. When he got closer, I saw he was a white man. He was making very little progress against the wind. When he got opposite, I hailed him. The words came back, "Are you George Clark?" "Yes!" He crossed over. He was an old acquaintance, Harry Hussey. He, like myself, could not stay away from the Colorado. I had not seen him for two years. During that time he had been in Africa, India, and several other parts of the world, and three months ago he and his brother (who had also been here) parted in London. His brother went to western Australia, and he came

Looking across the Colorado River to Yuma, Arizona, ca. 1900. The steamboat *St. Vallier* is docked at the Yuma landing at left. Southwest Museum, Highland Park, Los Angeles, California.

back to nowhere. It required two days to compare notes, then we took opposite directions.

That night I arrived at the city of Ehrenberg [125 miles upstream from Yuma]. Once, not many years ago, Ehrenberg was a place of consequence. Ships used to come around from San Francisco (and other parts of the world) to the mouth of the Colorado River and discharge their cargo on river steamers which brought it up the river to Ehrenberg (and other small places). It was then loaded on freight wagons and hauled to Prescott, Phoenix, Tucson, San Bernardino, and other parts. Then Ehrenberg flourished and had a population of over 2,000. Now Prescott, Phoenix, and all those places have railroads. The ships have stopped coming to the river—there is no freight to haul.[6] The teams were driven to other parts, sold, or left to a lingering death by starvation. The people disappeared, one by one, and today Ehrenberg is fighting hard to keep its name off the death record. In front of the houses where once children played lies the remains of freight wagons—a hub here and a tire there. Still, the inhabitants are not all gone. There is still a store run by Mr. Thomas Hamilton. He is postmaster, justice of the peace, runs a blacksmith shop and a ferryboat. After passing one night, I passed on.

The next 100 miles was not inhabited, but every now and then the old wall of a house could be seen on a mesa or tableland, which showed someone had mistaken dross for gold and, after finding his mistake, had packed his burros again to explore other regions, leaving his house to return no more. There it stands like a tomb, and will stand for they are all made of earth, and earth cannot decay.

Later on Norton's Landing was passed. It is also on the verge of the grave. Picacho still lives.[7] I passed there at sundown and at 12 today [January 8, 1897] tied up at Yuma,[8] a poorer but wiser man. The trip is ended—1,685 miles of passing scenery gone! I am now ready for another trip, but before I go farther south, I guess I had better hesitate a moment at least.

# NOTES

## Chapter 1

1. George Flavell begins his *Log of the Panthon* on August 30 after four days of floating down the Green River. He and his companion, Ramón Montéz, are camped in the upper part of Red Canyon (in Utah), about 84 miles downstream from their starting point, the town of Green River, Wyoming (elevation 6,070 feet), a station on the Union Pacific Railroad.

2. No mention of the name Dolores Canyon has been found in the literature pertaining to the upper Green River, nor is the name to be found on maps of the area. However, the name Dolores Canyon was undoubtedly in use by the local people at the time of Flavell's trip. About 70 miles downstream from the town of Green River, Wyoming, and about three miles downstream from the Wyoming–Utah state line, the river left a relatively open country and entered a canyon region through which it flowed for about 40 miles. The first 10 miles of this reach was made up of three small canyons: Flaming Gorge, Horseshoe Canyon, and Kingfisher Canyon. These canyons were without significant rapids. The river then flowed for about a mile through an open pocket known as Hideout Flat, then flowed easterly for about 29 miles through Red Canyon. Upon leaving Red Canyon, the Green meanders for about 34 miles through an open valley known as Brown's Park which sits astride the Utah–Colorado state line. At the foot of Brown's Park is the entrance to the fearsome Canyon of Lodore. In 1962 Flaming Gorge Dam was completed at about the midpoint of Red Canyon. The Green River is now inundated by the waters of Flaming Gorge Reservoir to within about five miles of the town of Green River, Wyoming.

3. When Flavell's estimates of distances traveled differ significantly from those indicated by modern maps, more realistic figures will be noted.

4. While portaging these falls in 1869, members of the first Powell expedition noticed a partially illegible inscription on a rock: "Ashley 18__5." The renowned fur trader William Henry Ashley had led a band of beaver trappers down the upper Green River in boats made of bison skins stretched over wooden frames in 1825. Ashley and his men traversed Red, Lodore, Whirlpool, and Split Mountain canyons, the first white men known to do so. Major Powell and his comrades named the site Ashley Falls. This once impressive cataract is quiet now—it is located about two miles upstream from Flaming Gorge Dam and lies under hundreds of feet of impounded water.

5. In the Rocky Mountains, a small, sheltered valley or pocket of bottom land in a canyon was often called a "hole." A small, treeless valley or meadow surrounded by mountains or forest was often labeled a "park." The meanings of the two terms somewhat overlap.

6. Autumn was usually a time of relatively low flow on the unregulated Green and Colorado rivers; the highest flows usually occurred from April through July, the result of snow melting in the high mountains.

7. The river runners were still in Brown's Park (called Brown's Hole in earlier days), which is reportedly named for Baptiste Brown, an old-time mountain man. Brown's Hole was a favorite wintering ground and rendezvous point for mountain men during the heyday of the beaver trade in the early 1800s. In the 1890s the area was well known as a hideout of horse and cattle thieves. Today much of Brown's Park is a federal wildlife refuge.

8. Lodore Canyon was named by the members of the Powell expedition of 1869 after the cataract at Lodore, England, which was known to them through the poem, *The Way the Water Comes Down at Lodore* by Robert Southey. The canyon is short (17 miles) but contains some of the most dangerous rapids to be found anywhere. At the foot of Lodore Canyon the Yampa River (called Bear River in the early days) enters the Green from the east. There is an open place in the canyon at the junction of the rivers, a "hole" or "park" known as Echo Park, through which the Green River flows for about two miles. Past Echo Park the river flows west through Whirlpool Canyon (nine miles long) and reenters the State of Utah. The

river then flows for eight miles through an open area called Island Park and then enters Split Mountain Canyon (seven miles long). Lodore, Whirlpool, and Split Mountain canyons are now within Dinosaur National Monument.

9. The Powell expedition lost a boat (the *No-Name*) in these rapids in 1869. The crew was saved, but the loss of the boat and the supplies it carried was still a "disaster" and the site was named accordingly.

10. Irish-born Patrick Lynch evidently took up residence at Echo Park in the late 1870s. The old hermit died in 1917 at the age of 88. He was finally granted his military pension a few years before his death. Echo Park is known locally as "Pat's Hole."

11. The village of Jensen, Utah (elevation 4,730 feet), is about 17 miles downstream from Split Mountain Canyon and about 200 miles downstream from Green River, Wyoming.

12. The adventurers were entering Desolation Canyon (about 80 miles long) which is followed immediately by Gray Canyon (about 26 miles long). Desolation and Gray canyons form a single gorge, but are differentiated on the basis of geology. The name Usher Canyon was doubtless a term in local use in Flavell's day.

13. The term "slow elk" is a euphemism used in the West to denote beef that has been acquired under dubious circumstances.

14. The town of Green River, Utah (elevation 4,050 feet), is about 11 miles downstream from Gray Canyon, 25 miles upstream from Labyrinth Canyon, and about 385 miles downstream from Green River, Wyoming. The Rio Grande Western Railroad, completed in 1883, crosses the Green River here, linking western Colorado with central Utah. Owing to the presence of the railroad, the town of Green River (initially called Blake) became a supply point for ranches and mines in the canyon country of southeastern Utah.

*Chapter 2*

1. The Auger Riffle, located about five miles downstream from the town of Green River, is not much of a rapid compared with those already run by Flavell and Montéz.

2. From the mid-1880s through the early 1900s there was considerable interest in mining placer gold on the lower Green River, on the Colorado River in Glen Canyon, at Lee's Ferry, and at several points on the Colorado below the Grand Canyon. Some of these

operations were quite ambitious and employed large steam-powered (or steam-electric) shovels and dredges. The hoped-for riches proved to be illusive, however, and large-scale placer mining was gone from the region by the beginning of World War I.

3. In 1891, the year after the Stanton survey was completed, John Hislop, William Edwards, and two other Stanton veterans joined a prospecting expedition financed by mining speculator James Best, with the purpose of examining some very remote sections of the Grand Canyon. Since the prospecting grounds were most easily accessed from the river, Best had two large boats built at Green River, Utah, stocked them with supplies, and the party of five prospectors headed down the Green. One of the boats was smashed in the ever-dangerous Cataract Canyon, and the party struggled on to Lee's Ferry in their remaining craft. There they abandoned the river and their hopes of finding gold in the Grand Canyon. The life preservers and rubber bags mentioned by Flavell were among the supplies discarded by the Best expedition. When at Lee's Ferry, Flavell does not mention finding any of this equipment.

4. The steamboat was the *Major Powell*, a small craft (length 35 feet, beam 8 feet) brought to Green River, Utah, by rail from Chicago in 1891. The boat was intended to carry excursion parties down the Green to Cataract Canyon and back, a round trip of some 240 miles. Over the next three years the *Major Powell*, with great difficulty, managed to make three of these trips. William H. Edwards was the pilot of the steamer on its last two excursions. Proving inadequate for these waters, her two six-horsepower steam engines were removed in 1894 and her hull left to rot in Green River Valley.

5. Flavell and Montéz had entered Labyrinth Canyon (about 60 miles long) which is followed immediately by Stillwater Canyon (about 32 miles long). Neither canyon contains dangerous rapids. Below Stillwater Canyon is the treacherous Cataract Canyon. Stillwater Canyon and the upper half of Cataract Canyon are now within Canyonlands National Park.

6. In Flavell's day the Colorado River began at the junction of the Green and Grand rivers at the head of Cataract Canyon. The name of the Grand River was changed to Colorado River by an act of Congress passed in 1921. The junction of the Green and the Grand (elevation 3,900 feet) is about 500 miles downstream from Green River, Wyoming.

7. Cataract Canyon (about 43 miles long) is followed by Narrow Canyon (10 miles long) and then the placid Glen Canyon (about 150 miles long). The lower half of Cataract Canyon and all of Narrow and Glen canyons are now submerged beneath the waters of Lake Powell. The lake is formed by Glen Canyon Dam which was completed in 1963. The dam is located in Arizona about 15 miles upstream from Lee's Ferry and about 150 miles downstream from Hite, Utah.

8. During the decade prior to Flavell and Montéz' odyssey, prospecting parties had occasionally attempted to float through Cataract Canyon in search of hidden riches. Ill-equipped and without skilled boatmen, these expeditions routinely met with disaster and many lives were lost. See: "The History of Cataract Canyon" in *Through the Grand Canyon from Wyoming to Mexico* by Ellsworth L. Kolb, 1914, pp. 341–343.

9. The mysterious animals could have been pronghorn, but the presence of these open-country animals at the bottom of Cataract Canyon is highly unlikely. It is more likely that they were female bighorn sheep, which have horns similar to those described by Flavell. In the late 1800s there was an erroneous belief held by many Southwesterners, including some seasoned backwoodsmen, that two species of hoofed mammals lived in the rocky crags of the mountains: "mountain sheep" and "ibex." The bighorn rams with their large horns usually were the mountain sheep; the bighorn ewes with their small horns usually were the ibex. Members of Powell's first expedition managed to bag two "mountain sheep" in Cataract Canyon in 1869.

10. Evidently Ramón was not good at timing boats; 600 yards in half a minute is equivalent to 42 miles per hour, far faster than the flow of the Colorado. The violent turbulence of the rapids creates the illusion that a boat is traveling much faster than it really is. At medium and low flows ($<$30,000 cubic feet per second), the maximum speed achieved by a boat floating down the Colorado River is probably no more than 10 miles per hour (15 feet per second).

11. The men were probably forced to line their boat through the "Big Drop," the worst rapid in a canyon full of deadly ones. The Big Drop is about 15 miles downstream from the confluence of the Green and Grand rivers.

12. A prospector named Cass Hite reportedly discovered a

"dandy crossing" of the Colorado River at the head of Glen Canyon in 1883. He was soon joined by brothers Ben and John, and John's son Homer, and the Hites operated a ferry at the crossing and worked placer claims in the vicinity for many years. Hite is now under the waters of Lake Powell.

13. This is undoubtedly the same J. W. "Jack" Wilson that Robert B. Stanton first met at Hite in 1889. The official postmaster for Hite in 1896 was Homer Hite and Mr. Wilson was evidently minding the store while Homer was away. Stanton returned to Glen Canyon in 1897 and for the next four years fought a losing battle trying to relieve the sands in the canyon of their placer gold. Jack Wilson worked sporadically for Stanton and his Hoskaninni Company during this time.

14. Lee's Ferry (elevation 3,110 feet) is located at the head of Marble Canyon, about 28 miles downstream from the Utah–Arizona state line, and about 720 miles downstream from Green River, Wyoming. John D. Lee, a fugitive from the law, established a ferry here in 1871. Lee was executed in 1877 for his part in the infamous Mountain Meadows Massacre of 1857 in which some 120 emmigrants were killed in southwestern Utah by Indians and Mormon fanatics. The ferryman met by Flavell was James Emett who had replaced Warren Johnson at Lee's Ferry earlier in the year. Evidently Emett's family had not yet arrived at this lonely outpost on the Colorado. Like John Lee, both Johnson and Emett were Mormons and practicing polygamists. Navajo Bridge, located four miles downstream, replaced the ferry in 1929.

15. The Kaibab Plateau, still famous for its mule deer herd, was called Buckskin Mountain by Mormon pioneers who found good deer hunting there.

16. The river runners would soon be entering Marble Canyon, the upper part of that great gorge known as the Grand Canyon. This will be the longest reach of unbroken canyon of their entire trip—about 277 miles from Lee's Ferry to the Grand Wash Cliffs. This part of the Colorado River affords the most spectacular white water boating to be found on the globe. Geographical features mentioned by Flavell will be identified in notes, when possible, and their location in "miles downstream from Lee's Ferry" will be given. The Grand Canyon is now within Grand Canyon National Park and the Hualapai Indian Reservation.

## Chapter 3

1. Soap Creek Rapid was first successfully run in 1927 by members of the Clyde Eddy expedition.

2. From about mile 20 to mile 29, the Colorado is choked with numerous rapids. This stretch of river is sometimes called "The Roaring Twenties."

3. The term "float" ("float ore") refers to pieces of rock that have been moved some distance from their place of origin by gravity or water. George Flavell's comments concerning the geology of the Grand Canyon are those of a perceptive, but, of course, untrained observer. For an up-to-date introduction to Grand Canyon geology see Collier, 1980. For a more detailed treatment of the subject see Breed and Roat, 1974.

4. The men had visited Stanton's Cave, located on the right bank of the river at about mile 32. After losing three of their party to drowning in July, 1889, the remainder of the Stanton surveying expedition cached their equipment in this cave, and climbed out of Marble Canyon. They retrieved their cache the next January. The piece of rope found by Flavell was likely a relic of the ill-fated Stanton survey.

5. An illustration included in Robert B. Stanton's article, "Through the Grand Cañon of the Colorado," published in *Scribner's Magazine* in November, 1890, depicts "Some ancient cliff dwellings in Marble Canyon." There are some small pre-Columbian Indian ruins in the canyon, but they are not conspicuous from the river.

6. The completion of the transcontinental railroad across northern Arizona in 1883 brought the South Rim of the Grand Canyon within fairly easy reach of visitors. One of the first to exploit the Canyon as a tourist attraction was "Captain" John Hance. He built a log "hotel" near Grandview Point and received his first guests in 1884. In 1894 Hance built a trail from the rim down Red Canyon to the river, the second trail he had built in the Grand Canyon. The trail reached the canyon bottom at the head of a vicious rapid, now known as Hance Rapid. The trail was for the use of his guests—others were supposed to pay a toll to travel on New Hance Trail. John Hance sold his tourist camp in 1895, but he continued to live at the South Rim for many years.

7. George Washington White was president of the University of California at Los Angeles from 1895 to 1899.

8. Bighorn sheep are still common in the Grand Canyon, particularly in the middle and lower reaches (i.e. downstream from about mile 100).

9. Before the regulation of the flow of the Colorado River by Glen Canyon Dam began in 1963, and subsequent changes in the character of some of the rapids downstream occurred, Lava Falls Rapid was acknowledged to be the worst rapid in the Grand Canyon. George Flavell must have become inured to danger to not make more mention of this maelstrom of foaming water. Lava Falls Rapid was not again run successfully until Buzz Holmstrom accomplished the feat in 1938.

10. This small marsh is located on the left bank of the river just below Lava Falls Rapid (mile 179). Highly mineralized springs (Warm Springs) discharge their water here, and evaporation leaves the rocks and vegetation encrusted with calcium carbonate and other salts.

11. This was probably an encampment of Southern Paiute Indians. The Powell expedition found (and plundered) some small Indian fields of corn and squash in this vicinity in 1869.

12. Lava Cliff Rapid (Spencer Canyon Rapid) was the last dangerous rapid in the Grand Canyon. Lava Cliff Rapid (mile 246) is now drowned out by Lake Mead which, when full, extends upriver to about mile 236. The lake is formed by Hoover Dam located in Boulder Canyon, about 30 miles downstream from the mouth of the Virgin River, and about 110 miles downstream from Lava Cliff Rapid. Hoover Dam was completed in 1935.

13. The courageous rivermen had passed the Grand Wash Cliffs (277 miles downstream from Lee's Ferry and 1,000 miles downstream from Green River, Wyoming) and exited the Grand Canyon. The elevation of the river at this point is about 900 feet.

14. Flavell exaggerates the barrenness of the Grand Canyon a bit, but after his harrowing ordeal he is entitled to do some complaining. His remark concerning bats is amusing as he has just passed Bat Cave (mile 266) which houses such a large colony of bats that attempts were made in the 1950s to mine their guano on a commercial scale.

15. Lower Disaster Falls in the Canyon of Lodore is now run on a routine basis by experienced boatmen using modern equipment. However, the shelf that stymied Flavell and Montéz does not often hamper today's boatmen. The shelf is only a problem at

very low flows—flows that have been rarely achieved since the regulation of the Green River by Flaming Gorge Dam began in 1962.

16. Lava Falls Rapid (mile 179 in the Grand Canyon) has a total fall of about 37 feet; throughout the journey, Flavell's estimates of distance, height, etc., were usually quite accurate.

## Chapter 4

1. The placer mining camp at Temple Bar was located on the Arizona side of the river (Nevada being on the north side of the Colorado), about 40 miles downstream from Grand Wash Cliffs. The large gravel bar took its name from a nearby butte which was thought to resemble a temple. The site is now a boat landing on Lake Mead.

2. The mouth of the Virgin River is about 10 miles downstream from Temple Bar and about 440 miles upstream from Yuma, Arizona. In Flavell's day, there were a few Mormon settlers on the lower Virgin River in Nevada, near its junction with the Colorado. The lower Virgin River is now under the waters of Lake Mead.

3. Needles, California (elevation 470 feet), is about 280 miles upstream from Yuma and about 1,200 miles downstream from Green River, Wyoming. The town is named for some sharp peaks (The Needles) about 15 miles downstream. Needles is a station on the Atchison, Topeka and Santa Fe Railroad.

4. The agency for the Colorado River Indian Reservation (established in 1865) is located near the present-day town of Parker, Arizona (elevation 350 feet), and is about 200 miles upstream from Yuma. The reservation serves primarily the Mohave and Chemehuevi tribes.

5. The Pullman–American Railway Union strike paralyzed commerce for several weeks during the summer of 1894, and was finally put down with the aid of federal troops.

6. Steamboat traffic on the lower Colorado River declined with the coming of the railroads in the late 1870s and early 1880s, and was effectively terminated in 1909 by the construction of Laguna Dam 14 miles upstream from Yuma. Since that time seven additional dams have been built on the river below the Grand Canyon, some to generate power, others to divert the waters of the Colorado to thirsty farms and cities. Today much of the Colorado Delta is farmed and, except during unusual periods of flood, only a trickle

of the flow of the river escapes the diversion canals and reaches the Gulf.

7. The small river settlements of Ehrenberg and Norton's Landing (in Arizona), and Picacho (in California), all became ghost towns shortly after the turn of the century.

8. The town of Yuma, Arizona (elevation 125 feet), is about 150 miles upstream from the Gulf of California, and about 1,500 miles downstream from Green River, Wyoming. Yuma is a station on the Southern Pacific Railroad.

# SELECTED BIBLIOGRAPHY

Babbitt, Bruce, 1978. *Grand Canyon: An Anthology.* Flagstaff, AZ: Northland Press.

Bartlett, Richard A., 1962. *Great Surveys of the American West.* Norman, OK: University of Oklahoma Press.

Belknap, Bill and Buzz Belknap, 1974. *Canyonlands River Guide.* Boulder City, NV: Westwater Books.

Belknap, Buzz, 1969. *Grand Canyon River Guide.* Boulder City, NV: Westwater Books.

Birdseye, Claude H. and Raymond Moore, 1924. "A Boat Voyage Through the Grand Canyon of the Colorado." *Geographical Review* (April), pp. 177–196.

Breed, William J. and Evelyn Roat, eds., 1974. *Geology of the Grand Canyon.* Flagstaff, AZ: Museum of Northern Arizona and Grand Canyon Natural History Association.

Collier, Michael, 1980. *An Introduction to Grand Canyon Geology.* Grand Canyon: Grand Canyon Natural History Association.

Crampton, C. Gregory, 1959. *Outline History of the Glen Canyon Region, 1776–1922.* University of Utah Anthropological Papers, No. 42. Salt Lake City: University of Utah Press.

———, 1964. *Historical Sites in Cataract and Narrow Canyons, and in Glen Canyon to California Bar.* University of Utah Anthropological Papers, No. 72. Salt Lake City: University of Utah Press.

———, 1964. *Standing Up Country: The Canyonlands of Utah and Arizona.* New York: Alfred A. Knopf and the University of Utah Press.

———, 1972. *Land of Living Rock: The Grand Canyon and High Plateaus.* New York: Alfred A. Knopf.

Crumbo, Kim, 1981. *A River Runner's Guide to the History of the*

*Grand Canyon*. Boulder, CO: Johnson Books.

Darrah, William C., 1951. *Powell of the Colorado*. Princeton, NJ: Princeton University Press.

———, and others, 1947. "The Exploration of the Colorado River in 1869." *Utah Historical Quarterly* (January–December), pp. 1–270.

———, and others, 1969. "John Wesley Powell and the Colorado River: Centennial Edition." *Utah Historical Quarterly* (Spring), pp. 146–283.

Dellenbaugh, Fredrick S., 1902. *The Romance of the Colorado River*. New York: G. P. Putnam's Sons.

———, 1908. *A Canyon Voyage*. New York: G. P. Putnam's Sons.

Eddy, Clyde, 1929. *Down the World's Most Dangerous River*. New York: Frederick A. Stokes.

Euler, Robert C., 1972. *The Paiute People*. Phoenix: Indian Tribal Series.

———, ed., 1984. *The Archaeology, Geology, and Paleobiology of Stanton's Cave, Grand Canyon National Park, Arizona*. Grand Canyon: Grand Canyon Natural History Association (Monograph No. 6).

Evans, Laura and Buzz Belknap, 1973. *Dinosaur River Guide*. Boulder City, NV: Westwater Books.

———, 1974. *Desolation River Guide*. Boulder City, NV: Westwater Books.

Fradkin, Philip L., 1981. *A River No More: The Colorado River and the West*. New York: Alfred A. Knopf.

Freeman, Lewis R., 1923. *The Colorado River, Yesterday, Today, and Tomorrow*. New York: Dodd, Mead.

———, 1924a. "Surveying the Grand Canyon of the Colorado." *National Geographic Magazine* (May), pp. 471–530, 547–548.

———, 1924b. *Down the Grand Canyon*. London: William Heineman.

Goldwater, Barry, 1941. "An Odyssey of the Green and Colorado: The Intimate Journal of Three Boats and Nine People on a Trip Down Two Rivers." *Arizona Highways* (January), pp. 6–13.

———, 1970. *Delightful Journey Down the Green and Colorado Rivers*. Tempe, AZ: Arizona Historical Foundation.

Gregory, Herbert E., ed., 1939. "Diary of Almon Harris Thompson, Geographer, Explorations of the Colorado River of the West and Its Tributaries, 1871–1875." *Utah Historical Quarterly* (January), pp. 3–140.

————, and others, 1948–49. "The Exploration of the Colorado River and the High Plateaus of Utah in 1871–72." *Utah Historical Quarterly* (January 1948–December 1949), pp. 1–540.

Grinnell, Joseph, 1914. "An Account of the Mammals and Birds of the Lower Colorado Valley, with Especial Reference to the Distributional Problems Presented." *University of California Publications in Zoology* (Vol. 12, No. 4), pp. 51–294.

Hansen, Wallace R., 1969. *The Geologic Story of the Uinta Mountains.* U.S. Geological Survey Bulletin 1291. Washington, D.C.: Government Printing Office.

Hoffmeister, Donald F., 1971. *Mammals of the Grand Canyon.* Urbana, IL: University of Illinois Press.

Hughes, J. Donald, 1978. *In the House of Stone and Light: A Human History of the Grand Canyon.* Grand Canyon: Grand Canyon Natural History Association.

James, George W., 1900. *In and Around the Grand Canyon.* Boston: Little, Brown.

Jones, Ann Trinkle and Robert C. Euler, 1979. *A Sketch of Grand Canyon Prehistory.* Grand Canyon: Grand Canyon Natural History Association.

Kolb, Ellsworth L., 1914. *Through the Grand Canyon from Wyoming to Mexico.* New York: Macmillan.

LaRue, E. C., 1916. *Colorado River and Its Utilization.* U.S. Geological Survey Water-Supply Paper 395. Washington, D.C.: Government Printing Office.

————, 1925. *Water Power and Flood Control of Colorado River Below Green River, Utah.* U.S. Geological Survey Water-Supply Paper 556. Washington, D.C.: Government Printing Office.

Lavender, David, 1982. *Colorado River Country.* New York: E. P. Dutton.

————, 1985. *River Runners of the Grand Canyon.* Tucson: University of Arizona Press and the Grand Canyon Natural History Association.

Lingenfelter, Richard E., 1978. *Steamboats on the Colorado, 1852–1916.* Tucson: University of Arizona Press.

Lohman, S. W., 1974. *The Geologic Story of Canyonlands National Park.* U.S. Geological Survey Bulletin 1327. Washington, D.C.: Government Printing Office.

McGee, W. J., 1898. "The Seri Indians." *Seventeenth Annual Report of the Bureau of American Ethnology, Part 1.* Washington, D.C.:

Government Printing Office, pp. 1–344.

McMechen, Edgar C., 1942. "The Hermit of Pat's Hole." *Colorado Magazine* (May), pp. 91–98.

Marston, Otis, 1960. "River Runners: Fast Water Navigation." *Utah Historical Quarterly* (July), pp. 290–307.

————, 1969. "Early Travel on the Green and Colorado Rivers." *The Smoke Signal* (No. 20). Tucson: Tucson Corral of the Westerners, pp. 231–236.

————, 1972. *Master Mariner.* Unpublished manuscript, Marston Collection, Huntington Library, San Marino, CA.

Morgan, Dale L., 1964. *The West of William Ashley.* Denver: Old West.

North, Mary R., 1930. *Down the Colorado.* New York, London: G. P. Putnam's Sons.

Ohmart, Robert D., 1979. *Past and Present Biotic Communities of the Lower Colorado River Mainstream and Selected Tributaries. Vol. 1: Davis Dam to Mexican Border.* Boulder City, NV: Bureau of Reclamation.

Powell, John W., 1875. *Exploration of the Colorado River of the West and Its Tributaries.* Washington, D.C.: Government Printing Office.

————, 1895. *Canyons of the Colorado.* Meadville, PA: Flood and Vincent.

Purdy, William M., 1959. *An Outline of the History of the Flaming Gorge Area.* University of Utah Anthropological Papers, No. 37. Salt Lake City: University of Utah Press.

Rabbitt, Mary C., and others, 1969. *The Colorado River Region and John Wesley Powell.* U.S. Geological Survey Professional Paper 669. Washington, D.C.: Government Printing Office.

Rusho, W. L. and C. Gregory Crampton, 1975. *Desert River Crossing: Historic Lee's Ferry on the Colorado.* Salt Lake City: Peregrine Smith.

Stanton, Robert B., 1890. "Through the Grand Cañon of the Colorado." *Scribner's Magazine* (November), pp. 591–613.

————, 1932. *Colorado River Controversies.* Ed. by James Chalfant. New York: Dodd, Mead.

————, 1961. *The Hoskaninni Papers: Mining in Glen Canyon, 1897–1902.* Ed. by C. Gregory Crampton and Dwight L. Smith. University of Utah Anthropological Papers, No. 54. Salt Lake City: University of Utah Press.

————, 1965. *Down the Colorado.* Ed. by Dwight L. Smith. Norman, OK: University of Oklahoma Press.

Stegner, Wallace, 1953. *Beyond the Hundredth Meridian: John Wesley Powell and the Second Opening of the West.* Boston: Houghton Mifflin.

————, ed., 1955. *This Is Dinosaur: Echo Park Country and Its Magic Rivers.* New York: Alfred A. Knopf.

Stevens, Larry, 1983. *The Colorado River in Grand Canyon: A Guide.* Flagstaff, AZ: Red Lake Books.

Stone, Julius F., 1932. *Canyon Country: The Romance of a Drop of Water and a Grain of Sand.* New York: G. P. Putnam's Sons.

Sykes, Godfrey, 1937. *The Colorado Delta.* American Geographical Society Special Publication No. 19. Washington, D.C.: Carnegie Institution and the American Geographical Society of New York.

Turner, Raymond M. and Martin M. Karpiscak, 1980. *Recent Vegetation Changes Along the Colorado River Between Glen Canyon Dam and Lake Mead, Arizona.* U.S. Geological Survey Professional Paper 1132. Washington, D.C.: Government Printing Office.

U.S. Bureau of Reclamation, 1946. *The Colorado River: A Natural Menace Becomes a National Resource.* Washington, D.C.: Government Printing Office.

Wooley, Ralf R., 1930. *The Green River and Its Utilization.* U.S. Geological Survey Water-Supply Paper 618. Washington, D.C.: Government Printing Office.

Zwinger, Ann, 1975. *Run, River, Run.* New York: Harper and Row.

# INDEX